wild reckoning

wild reckoning

an anthology provoked by
Rachel Carson's *Silent Spring*

edited by John Burnside and Maurice Riordan

 CALOUSTE GULBENKIAN FOUNDATION

Published by the
Calouste Gulbenkian Foundation
United Kingdom Branch
98 Portland Place
London WIB IET
Tel: 020 7908 7604
Email: info@gulbenkian.org.uk
Website: www.gulbenkian.org.uk

Introduction and this selection © 2004 John Burnside and Maurice
Riordan
Foreword © 2004 Jonathan Bate
Poems commissioned for this anthology © 2004 Simon Armitage,
John Burnside, Mark Doty, Paul Farley, Allison Funk, Linda
Gregerson, Seamus Heaney, James Lasdun, Andrew Motion, Paul
Muldoon, Eiléan Ní Chuilleanáin, Deryn Rees-Jones, Christopher
Reid, Maurice Riordan, Robin Robertson, Michael Symmons
Roberts, Robert Wrigley
For copyright of all other poems see acknowledgements page 249.
The right of John Burnside and Maurice Riordan to be identified as
authors of the Introduction and editors of this work has been
asserted in accordance with the Copyright, Designs and Patents Act
1988.

ISBN I 903080 00 2

British Library Cataloguing-in-Publication Data
A catalogue record for this book is available from the British Library

Designed by Helen Swansbourne
Typeset by Ferdinand Pageworks
Printed by Expression Printers Ltd, IP23 8HH

Distributed by Central Books, 99 Wallis Road, London E9 5LN
Tel: 0845 458 9911, Fax: 0845 458 9912,
Email: orders@centralbooks.com
Website: www.centralbooks.co.uk

Front cover: Doug and Mike Starn, *Attracted to Light film still #5*, 2003.
Lambda print mounted on aluminium, edition of 5, 112 x 87 cm.
Courtesy of the artists and Houldsworth Gallery, London.

Contemplating the teeming life of the shore, we have an uneasy sense of the communication of some universal truth that lies just beyond our grasp. What is the message signaled by the hordes of diatoms, flashing their microscopic lights in the night sea? What truth is expressed by the legions of the barnacles, whitening the rocks with their habitations, each small creature within finding the necessities of its existence in the sweep of the surf? And what is the meaning of so tiny a being as the transparent wisp of protoplasm that is a sea lace, existing for some reason inscrutable to us — a reason that demands its presence by the trillion amid the rocks and weeds of the shore? The meaning haunts and ever eludes us, and in its very pursuit we approach the ultimate mystery of Life itself.

Rachel Carson, *The Edge of the Sea* (1956)

Contents

Foreword

One of the central books of the ancient world is *The Greek Anthology*. It is a collection of lyrical poems that sets the pattern for all subsequent poetry anthologies. Anthology: the second half of the word comes from the Greek for words (*logoi*), the first from the Greek for flowers (*anthoi*). An anthology is a gathering of flowers.

The work of the poet is to use words with care, precision and love in order to make us see the world more clearly. 'To see a world in a grain of sand', as William Blake has it, 'And a heaven in a wild flower.' When you read a good poem with the attention that it deserves, you 'Hold infinity in the palm of your hand, / And eternity in an hour.'

Blake could take eternity for granted. For the older poets in this gathering of flowers – from the riddler of the Anglo-Saxon Exeter Book through the craggy northern Gawain poet to the Romantics and beyond – nature was a sign of stability and permanence against which the instability and transience of human things could be measured. They recognised that nature was in a perpetual state of change but – following Pythagoras – they regarded flux or metamorphosis as itself a kind of constancy.

We cannot take the eternity of nature for granted. In *Silent Spring* Rachel Carson asked us to imagine a world without birdsong. Such, she feared, was the world being made by pesticides. It is testimony to the prophetic power of her book that it should have inspired some remarkable new poetry in this one, whilst also casting new light back on a rich array of older poetry. A world without birdsong would be like a world without poets, which may be why so many of the major poets of our time have come to see that theirs is an ecological art. As anthology is the *logos* of the *anthos*, the flower, so ecology is the *logos* of the *oikos* – the home, the dwelling-place, the earth.

JONATHAN BATE

Introduction

'Nature offers no home'
James P. Carse, *Finite and Infinite Games* (1986)

In the public gardens where the children are playing there is a grove of maple trees which, early this bright autumnal morning, are as rich in colour as they've ever been. Scarlet, gold, crimson – the gorgeous spectacle these trees put on from year to year is a thing of beauty and a joy for as long as autumn lasts. But that beauty is not accidental, it is a strategy – an act, one might say, of intelligence. Recent research has suggested that some deciduous trees use these bright colours as protection against predators:

> Most people's response to trees' autumnal colours is 'wow'. Two biologists at the University of Oxford have instead asked 'why?' Their answer: the trees are sending the message 'pick on someone else' to their insect enemies. Sam Brown and the late William Hamilton have found that the tree species with most to lose to aphids shout the loudest, putting on the brightest red and yellow displays. Maples, for example, which are renowned for their spectacular colours, are some of the most heavily aphid-infested trees.
>
> In autumn, trees make a wide range of red, yellow and purple pigments. Most research has focused on how and when these colours are produced. But Brown says that 'the diversity of colour changes demanded an explanation'. The duo compared published descriptions of aphid diets and autumn leaves. Aphids are choosy about what they eat and are very sensitive to colour. The damage aphids can inflict also gives trees a strong incentive to deter their attentions. Hamilton and Brown have proposed that vivid leaves are a 'handicap signal'. By blowing its resources on showing off, a tree flaunts its health and commitment to defence. A sycamore aphid looking for a place to spend the winter and reproduce next year would steer clear of sycamore dazzlers and head for the dullards.[1]

This story illustrates our varied and often conflicting attitudes to nature. On the one hand, the natural world is a repository of beauty, a source of continuing wonder, even of mystery. On the other, it is a matter for scientific investigation, a puzzle to be explained by the application of reason and informed observation. For some, nature is a church, or a pagan temple; for others, an inexhaustible laboratory. In Western culture, especially since the Romantic period, the two positions have been placed as opposites: where poets saw beauty, form, even the divine in nature, scientists observed data, function, the laws of physics. More recently, however, the viewpoints have been moving towards a common appreciation of nature, where function and form, beauty and objective fact, the laws of nature and a sense of mystery can coexist. The poet Robert Wrigley acknowledges this tendency when he says the song of a meadowlark 'sounds to me like reason'; [2] Loren Eiseley, the University of Pennsylvania's Franklin Professor of Anthropology and the History of Science at the time of his death, could contend, in his last collection of essays, that:

> 'Natural' is a magician's word – and like all such entities, it should be used sparingly lest there arise from it, as now, some unglimpsed, unintended world, some monstrous caricature called into being by the indiscreet articulation of worn syllables. Perhaps, if we are wise, we will prefer to stand like those forgotten humble creatures who poured little gifts of flint into a grave. Perhaps there may come to us then, in some such moment, a ghostly sense that an invisible doorway has been opened – a doorway which, widening out, will take man beyond the nature that he knows. [3]

Poets and life scientists are not strangers, of course. Both must use language to express their understanding of the phenomena of the world. Both feel the need for precision and elegance in their works. Yet there have been times of needless opposition, from the Enlightenment faith in 'objectivity', on the one side, to the insistence that 'we murder to dissect' on the other. Yet, increasingly, we have been able to speak across the divide and, while we do not always agree in emphasis, we do share a common understanding that intelligence has to do with the making of connections, with the linking of one thing with another, in order to apprehend a greater whole.

Perhaps the writer whose work most clearly embodies both this necessary accord and the continuing debate between the rational and a sense of magic is Rachel Carson. The most lyrical – and, it has to be said, most persuasively magical – of science writers, Carson nevertheless possessed true rigour and a delicate, clear-thinking logic that her opponents in the pharmaceutical and agrochemical businesses came to fear. Nobody wrote more beautifully about the environment – writing about the sea, for example, she has no recent equal – yet she came to be known, for her own generation and for those that followed, as a passionate environmental activist. In the twentieth century, it had become customary to say that scientists had no social role, nor any social responsibility, just as a generation of poets came to believe that 'poetry makes nothing happen'. Carson challenged both these assumptions. The scientist cannot simply do the experiments and leave the resulting applications to the politicians; the writer cannot hide from his or her social obligations in an ivory tower of form and allusion. All of us, writers and artists, biologists and technicians, have a duty to the natural world, and to all those others – human, animal and vegetable – who share it. Our vision must be larger than our given field; it must be – in the full sense of the word – intelligent. We cannot belong to one thing and not another. To belong, as Rachel Carson knew, is to belong to everything, to be part of an uninterrupted whole. To belong, to make ourselves at home in this world, is the most intelligent thing we can do; it is also the most difficult.

Rachel Carson did not want to write *Silent Spring*, the book for which she is now best known. True, she was painfully aware of the indiscriminate use of pesticides and had proposed articles on the problem to the magazines she was writing for as far back as the late forties, but *Silent Spring* was in many ways not her kind of project. In her great sea trilogy, *Under the Sea Wind* (1941), *The Sea Around Us* (1951), and *The Edge of the Sea* (1956), a singular voice emerges, at once precise and lyrical, a voice she had come to know as her own. It was not the polemical voice for a 'crusading' book on DDT. By 1957, however, the pesticide problem was alarming, as an attempt to prevent 'an infestation of gypsy moths' in the city of New York clearly demonstrated:

> The gypsy moth [Carson wrote] is a forest insect, certainly not an inhabitant of cities. Nor does it live in meadows, cultivated fields, gardens or marshes. Nevertheless, the planes hired by the United States Department of Agriculture and the New York Department of Agriculture and Markets showered down the prescribed DDT-in-fuel-oil with impartiality. They sprayed truck gardens and dairy farms, fish ponds and salt marshes. They sprayed the quarter-acre lots of suburbia, drenching a housewife making a desperate effort to cover her garden before the roaring plane reached her, and showering insecticide over children at play and commuters at railway stations. At Setauket a fine quarter horse drank from a trough in a field which the planes had sprayed; ten hours later it was dead.[4]

This was probably the single event that most decided Carson to write *Silent Spring*. She had hoped to find a more suitable person to take the book on, an investigative journalist, ideally, who could weave together all the diverse strands of anecdotal and scientific evidence, political background and shady manoeuvring. When nobody emerged she set to work, knowing that it would cost her far too much in time and effort. But 'there would be no peace for me', she said, 'if I kept silent.'

It would be a mistake, however, to see *Silent Spring* simply as a book about pesticides, even if that was how it was quickly characterised by its opponents, who wanted to portray Carson as anti-chemicals and hence anti-progress. In fact, some of Carson's best writing goes into the book, as she carries her readers along with the argument. Most of all, she wanted people to see the background to the problem of DDT, as in this passage, where she discusses agriculture and business:

> We are told that the enormous and expanding use of pesticides is necessary to maintain farm production. Yet is our real problem not one of over-production? Our farms, despite measures to remove acreages from production and to pay farmers not to produce, have yielded such a staggering excess of crops that the American taxpayer in 1962 is paying out more than one billion dollars a year as the total carrying cost of the surplus food storage programme. And is the situation helped when one branch of the Agriculture Department tries to reduce production while another states, as it did in 1958, 'It is believed generally that a reduction of crop acreages under provisions of the Soil Bank will stimulate interest in use of chemicals to obtain maximum production on the land retained in crops.'[5]

As the book progresses, Carson is a careful guide through the complex web of political and fiscal shenanigans, explaining to a public that would have known almost nothing about biological – as opposed to chemical – pest control exactly how government and other bodies manipulated the figures to make the biological option always seem 'too expensive'. In this alone, *Silent Spring* is a towering achievement: Carson makes the necessary case against DDT, but on the way she exposes the entire system. As Paul Brooks notes in his excellent study of her work, *The House of Life*, 'she was questioning not only the indiscriminate use of poisons but the basic irresponsibility of an industrialised, technological society toward the natural world'.[6]

Not surprisingly, the powers that be hated *Silent Spring*. But the public, and most of the popular press, loved it. It became a bestseller, a talking point in factories and drawing-rooms, the subject of hundreds of newspaper articles, parodies, cartoons and debates. More importantly, it reached the office of JFK, who asked his scientific adviser, Jerome B. Wiesner, to begin a study of the whole DDT question. A Pesticides Committee was set up and quickly produced a report criticising the chemical companies and endorsing Carson's views. Something had been achieved.

But only a little. Testifying to that same committee in June 1963, Rachel Carson took the opportunity to remind the world of the wider implications of her work:

> We still talk in terms of conquest. We still haven't become mature enough to think of ourselves as only a tiny part of a vast and incredible universe. Man's attitude toward nature is today critically important simply because we have now acquired a fateful power to alter and destroy nature. But man is part of nature and his war against nature is inevitably a war against himself.[7]

It is forty years since that statement. In the intervening years, some ground has been gained, but much has been lost. Spring has become a little more silent and all the seasons considerably noisier. A recent study concluded that the number of sparrows in Edinburgh's Princes Street Gardens was falling because the birds were unable to hear their own songs through the sound of traffic that roars daily through this and every other modern city. With their songs of courtship and territory disappearing, it is not simply that the birds can no longer breed; in a very real sense, they are no longer meaningfully there at all. They live in an Eraserhead world of background noise, haunted by the odd plaintive, half-heard whisper of fellowship. We might reasonably ask the question: what is a bird, if it can no longer hear its song? But – for us – a more alarming question also hangs in the shadows needing to be uttered: what does it mean to be human, in a world where birdsong is disappearing?

These questions arise because business and government have succeeded in keeping us all in two minds about ecology, as science, and as a workable philosophy. The most calculated criticisms of Carson made in the wake of *Silent Spring* were that she was 'mystical', or 'sentimental' – and somehow that view of ecology has stuck. Yet mystical and sentimental are exactly what ecology is not; these honours belong to the old religions of 'market values' and 'objectivity'. If Rachel Carson were alive today, she would be emphasising our need to understand how central ecology is to our lives. What she wanted to show us was not that everything was interconnected, as in some web or lattice – to use the current, popular cybernetics model – but that matter is continuous, like a Celtic knot. This continuum, she believed, was the one single narrative that includes all others. *Time* magazine, in its 1962 attack on *Silent Spring*, described her case as 'unfair, one-sided and hysterically over-emphatic. Many of the scary generalizations … are patently unsound. "It is not possible" says Miss Carson, "to add pesticides to water anywhere without threatening the purity of water everywhere". It takes only a moment of reflection to show that this is nonsense.' But *this* is exactly the point – you cannot pollute water locally. All waters come together, as all life does:

> Individual elements are lost to view, only to reappear again and again in different incarnations in a kind of material immortality. Kindred forces to those which, in some period inconceivably remote, gave birth to that primal bit of protoplasm tossing on the ancient seas continue their mighty and incomprehensible work. Against this cosmic background the life span of a particular plant or animal appears, not as a drama complete in itself, but only as a brief interlude in a panorama of endless change.[8]

Is this mysticism? If so, maybe we need more of it in our thinking. Some of us, however, have come to the conclusion that Carson's words are not only lyrical, but truly scientific. What her work proposes, and what it achieves, is a new form of ecology, a science of belonging, a science founded as much on appreciation and lyricism as on observation and precision – a science, then, that shares a lot of common ground with poetry.

The initial idea for *Wild Reckoning* was that it would be a book of poems commissioned from contemporary poets to celebrate the world that Rachel Carson loved and wrote about so persuasively. In 2002, the fortieth anniversary of the publication of *Silent Spring*, we found ourselves reflecting upon the fact that this wonderful writer and environmental activist was, in an important sense, neglected. During a public discussion of Carson's legacy, one speaker said that some writers' works are so intrinsic to the spirit of their age that their ideas become a part of our common currency and they no longer need to be read. This would be a great loss in the case of Rachel Carson. If this anthology serves just one purpose, it is to remind people of how much appreciated as a *writer* she was – a writer whose legacy, acknowledged or otherwise, is so integral to our thinking that while we scarcely notice its influence it informs our poetry at a fundamental level.

To celebrate that influence – that sense of the unity of living things, that wonderful marriage in one pen of lyricism and observation – we asked poets from both sides of the Atlantic to work directly with a scientist on, first, a dialogue, and second, a poem that related in some way to that scientist's area of expertise. What we were looking for wasn't 'nature poetry'. Instead, we sought out poets who, it seemed to us, had something vital to say about the human relationship with the natural world in the broadest sense: poets with a philosophical concern with the land; those whose work dealt, in a clear-sighted and compassionate fashion, with animal and plant life; poets whose lyrical explorations had to do with connection, continuity and the interlaced quality of all life.

It has to be said that we were more than fortunate in our choices – and we are grateful to the scientists and poets who agreed to contribute to this project. Alongside their work, we have set poems that seem to us to represent our great tradition of nature poetry at its most imaginative and original – poems that question and explore the relationship between the human and the non-human, and those poems that classically express, propose, or in some cases discover noble and enduring visions of that relationship. But, above all, we looked for poems that *sing out* that human experience of the varied earth in the most memorable way.

In making our selection (from which there are no doubt many unintended regrettable omissions) we determined not to gather together a garland of 'nice poems about birds and flowers'. It is worth remembering, for one thing, those park trees with which we began – whose exuberant colours delighted the eye this autumn in the early years of a new century. Does that bounty portend a disastrous change in climate? Our joy is tempered by the knowledge that, in all likelihood, careless human activity has already set the seasons in disarray. Therefore, we were conscious of an urgent need here to challenge the assumption that the principal subjects of nature poetry were matters green or objects furry, and return to the original meaning of the word ecology: that is, to its delineation of a *Logos* of dwelling, a *Logos* that is neither exclusively 'science' nor 'art', but side-steps such definitions in an attempt to understand, in the fullest sense, what it is to dwell in the world as humans. Of course, how we feel about what is usually seen as nature (trees, lizards, clouds, reindeer, meadows) is vitally important to our future as a species, but how we view nature is only part of a wider question. And that question is one of belonging, a reckoning, and an accommodation, with the world around us, where no home is offered, but everything – including the ultimate mystery of life itself – is shared.

JOHN BURNSIDE and MAURICE RIORDAN
Fife–London October 2003

---

1 John Whitfield, 'Trees tell pests to leaf off: Autumn colours might be a warning to insects', in *Nature*, 10 July 2001. 2 Robert Wrigley, 'Anecdotal Fencepost', from *Lives of the Animals* (New York, Penguin, 2003). 3 Loren Eiseley, 'How Natural is "Natural"', from *The Star Thrower* (New York, Times Books, 1978). 4 Rachel Carson, *Silent Spring* (Boston, Houghton Mifflin, 1962). 5 *Ibid.* 6 Paul Brooks, *The House of Life: Rachel Carson at Work* (Boston, Houghton Mifflin, 1972). 7 *Ibid.* 8 Rachel Carson, 'Undersea', in *Atlantic Monthly*, vol. 160, September 1937.

The Commissioned Poems

Seventeen of these poems were commissioned by the Calouste Gulbenkian Foundation to mark the fortieth anniversary of the publication of *Silent Spring* and represent a significant and, we hope, a ground-breaking collaboration between poets and scientists.

The poems are by Simon Armitage, John Burnside, Mark Doty, Paul Farley, Allison Funk, Linda Gregerson, Seamus Heaney, James Lasdun, Andrew Motion, Paul Muldoon, Eiléan Ní Chuilleanáin, Deryn Rees-Jones, Christopher Reid, Maurice Riordan, Robin Robertson, Michael Symmons Roberts, and Robert Wrigley. Special thanks are due to the scientists who gave so generously of their time and expertise: Sir David Attenborough; Dr Peter Bennett; Dr Elizabeth Cooper of the Norsk Polarinstutt, Tromso; Professor Richard Fortey of the Natural History Museum; Wildlife Rehabilitator Kristine Flones; David Funk of the Stroud Water Research Center in Avondale, Pennsylvania; Professor James O'Meara; Charles Robbins, Director of the Bear Research, Education and Conservation Program at Washington State University; Dr Tim Sparks of the Centre for Ecology and Hydrology; Sir John Sulston; Michael Walters, Emeritus Fellow and Curator of Eggs at the Natural History Museum; Professor Bernard Wood.

Thanks are also due to Jill Attenborough of the Woodland Trust; Aosaf Afzal of the Royal Society; Patrick MacEntee S.C.; Seámas MacPhilib of the National Museum in Dublin; Críostóir Mac Cárthaigh of the Department of Irish Folklore at University College Dublin; and Dr Jon Turney.

The editors are deeply grateful to Siân Ede, Louisa Hooper and Felicity Luard for their help with every aspect of the book, to Mary Ferdinand and Helen Swansbourne for the typesetting and design, and to Doug and Mike Starn and Houldsworth Gallery, London, for the cover image.

wild reckoning

RODNEY JONES

The Assault on the Fields

It was like snow, if snow could blend with air and hover,
    making, at first,
A rolling boil, mottling the pine thickets behind the fields,
    but then flattening
As it spread above the fenceposts and the whiteface cattle,
    an enormous, luminous tablet,

A shimmering, an efflorescence, through which my father
    rode on his tractor,
Masked like a Martian or a god to create the cloud where
    he kept vanishing;
Though, of course, it was not a cloud or snow, but poison,
    dichlorodiphenyltrichloroethane,

The word like a bramble of black locust on the tongue,
    and, after a while,
It would fill the entire valley, as, one night in spring,
    five years earlier,
A man from Joe Wheeler Electric had touched a switch
    and our houses filled with light.

Already some of the music from the radio went with me
    when the radio was off.
The bass, the kiss of the snare. Some of the thereness
    rubbing off on the hereness.
But home place still meant family. Misfortune was a well
    of yellowish sulfur water.

The Flowerses lived next door. Coyd drove a road grader
   for the county.
Martha baked, sewed, or cleaned, complaining beautifully
   of the dust
Covering her new Formica counters. Martha and Coyd,
   Coyd Jr., Linda, and Jenny.

How were they different from us? They owned
   a television,
Knew by heart each of the couples on Dick Clark's
   American Bandstand.
At dusk Junior, the terrible, would beat on a cracked
   and unfrettable Silvertone guitar

While he pitched from the top of his wayward voice
   one of a dozen songs
He'd written for petulant freshman girls. 'Little Patti,'
   'Matilda,'
'Sweet Bonnie G.' What did the white dust have to do
   with anything?

For Junior, that year, it was rock'n'roll; if not rock'n'roll,
   then abstract expressionism –
One painting comes back. Black frame. Black canvas –
   'I call it *Death*,' he would say,
Then stomp out onto the front lawn to shoot his .22 rifle
   straight into the sky above his head.

Surely if Joel Shapiro's installation of barbed wire and
   crumbled concrete blocks,
In a side room of the most coveted space in Manhattan,
   pays homage
To the most coveted space in Manhattan, then Junior
   Flowers's *Death*,

Hanging on a wall dingy with soot in North Alabama,
  is a comment, too.

Are they the same thing? I do not know that they are not
  the same thing.
And the white dust, so magical, so poisonous: how does it
  differ from snow?
As it thins gradually over many nights, we don't notice
  it; once the golden

Carp have rotted from the surfaces of ponds, there is no
  stench to it;
It is more of an absence of things barely apprehended,
  of flies, of moths;
Until one day the hawks who patrolled the air over
  the chicken coops are gone;

And when a woman, who was a girl then, finds a lump,
  what does it have to do
With the green fields and the white dust boiling
  and hovering?
When I think of the name Jenny Flowers, it is that
  whiteness I think of.

Some bits have fallen to clump against a sheet of tin
  roofing
The tornado left folded in the ditch, and she stoops there
  to gather
A handful of chalk to mark the grounds for hopscotch.

JOHN CLARE

The Moors

Far spread the moory ground, a level scene
Bespread with rush and one eternal green,
That never felt the rage of blundering plough,
Though centuries wreathed spring blossoms on its brow.
Autumn met plains that stretched them far away
In unchecked shadows of green, brown, and grey.
Unbounded freedom ruled the wandering scene;
No fence of ownership crept in between
To hide the prospect from the gazing eye;
Its only bondage was the circling sky.
A mighty flat, undwarfed by bush and tree,
Spread its faint shadow of immensity,
And lost itself, which seemed to eke its bounds,
In the blue mist the horizon's edge surrounds.

   Now this sweet vision of my boyish hours,
Free as spring clouds and wild as forest flowers,
Is faded all – a hope that blossomed free,
And hath been once as it no more shall be.
Enclosure came, and trampled on the grave
Of labour's rights, and left the poor a slave;
And memory's pride, ere want to wealth did bow,
Is both the shadow and the substance now.
The sheep and cows were free to range as then
Where change might prompt, nor felt the bonds of men.
Cows went and came with every morn and night
To the wild pasture as their common right;
And sheep, unfolded with the rising sun,
Heard the swains shout and felt their freedom won,

Tracked the red fallow field and heath and plain,
Or sought the brook to drink, and roamed again;
While the glad shepherd traced their tracks along,
Free as the lark and happy as her song.
But now all's fled, and flats of many a dye
That seemed to lengthen with the following eye,
Moors losing from the sight, far, smooth, and blea,
Where swopt the plover in its pleasure free,
Are banished now with heaths once wild and gay
As poet's visions of life's early day.
Like mighty giants of their limbs bereft,
The skybound wastes in mangled garbs are left,
Fence meeting fence in owner's little bounds
Of field and meadow, large as garden-grounds,
In little parcels little minds to please,
With men and flocks imprisoned, ill at ease.
For with the poor scared freedom bade farewell,
And fortune-hunters totter where they fell;
They dreamed of riches in the rebel scheme
And find too truly that they did but dream.

Going, Going

I thought it would last my time –
The sense that, beyond the town,
There would always be fields and farms,
Where the village louts could climb
Such trees as were not cut down;
I knew there'd be false alarms

In the papers about old streets
And split-level shopping, but some
Have always been left so far;
And when the old part retreats
As the bleak high-risers come
We can always escape in the car.

Things are tougher than we are, just
As earth will always respond
However we mess it about;
Chuck filth in the sea, if you must:
The tides will be clean beyond.
– But what do I feel now? Doubt?

Or age, simply? The crowd
Is young in the M1 café;
Their kids are screaming for more –
More houses, more parking allowed,
More caravan sites, more pay.
On the Business Page, a score

Of spectacled grins approve
Some takeover bid that entails
Five per cent profit (and ten
Per cent more in the estuaries): move
Your works to the unspoilt dales
(Grey area grants)! And when

You try to get near the sea
In summer ...
                It seems, just now,
To be happening so very fast;
Despite all the land left free
For the first time I feel somehow
That it isn't going to last,

That before I snuff it, the whole
Boiling will be bricked in
Except for the tourist parts –
First slum of Europe: a role
It won't be so hard to win,
With a cast of crooks and tarts.

And that will be England gone,
The shadows, the meadows, the lanes,
The guildhalls, the carved choirs.
There'll be books; it will linger on
In galleries; but all that remains
For us will be concrete and tyres.

Most things are never meant.
This won't be, most likely: but greeds
And garbage are too thick-strewn
To be swept up now, or invent
Excuses that make them all needs.
I just think it will happen, soon.

WILLIAM WORDSWORTH

On the Projected Kendal and Windermere Railway

Is then no nook of English ground secure
From rash assault? Schemes of retirement sown
In youth, and 'mid the busy world kept pure
As when their earliest flowers of hope were blown,
Must perish; – how can they this blight endure?
And must he too the ruthless change bemoan
Who scorns a false utilitarian lure
'Mid his paternal fields at random thrown?
Baffle the threat, bright Scene, from Orrest-head
Given to the pausing traveller's rapturous glance:
Plead for thy peace, thou beautiful romance
Of nature; and, if human hearts be dead,
Speak, passing winds; ye torrents, with your strong
And constant voice, protest against the wrong.

The Larch Grove

Line above line the nursling larches planted,
  Still as they climb with interspace more wide,
Let in and out the sunny beams that slanted,
  And shot and crankled down the mountain's side.

The larches grew, and darker grew the shade;
  And sweeter aye the fragrance of the Spring;
Pink pencils all the spiky boughs arrayed,
  And small green needles called the birds to sing.

They grew apace as fast as they could grow,
  As fain the tawny fell to deck and cover,
They haply thought to soothe the pensive woe,
  Or hide the joy of stealthy tripping lover.

Ah, larches! that shall never be your lot;
  Nought shall you have to do with amorous weepers,
Nor shall ye prop the roof of cozy cot,
  But rumble out your days as railway sleepers.

Trees at the Arctic Circle
(*Salix cordifolia* – Ground Willow)

They are 18 inches long
or even less
crawling under rocks
grovelling among the lichens
bending and curling to escape
making themselves small
finding new ways to hide
Coward trees
I am angry to see them
like this
not proud of what they are
bowing to weather instead
careful of themselves
worried about the sky
afraid of exposing their limbs
like a Victorian married couple

I call to mind great Douglas firs
I see tall maples waving green
and oaks like gods in autumn gold
the whole horizon jungle dark
and I crouched under that continual night
But these
even the dwarf shrubs of Ontario
mock them
Coward trees

And yet — and yet —
their seed pods glow
like delicate grey earrings
their leaves are veined and intricate
like tiny parkas
They have about three months
to make sure the species does not die
and that's how they spend their time
unbothered by any human opinion
just digging in here and now
sending their roots down down down
And you know it occurs to me
                about 2 feet under
those roots must touch permafrost
ice that remains ice forever
and they use it for their nourishment
they use death to remain alive

I see that I've been carried away
in my scorn of the dwarf trees
most foolish in my judgments
To take away the dignity
                of any living thing
even tho it cannot understand
                the scornful words
is to make life itself trivial
and yourself the Pontifex Maximus
                of nullity
I have been stupid in a poem
I will not alter the poem
but let the stupidity remain permanent
as the trees are
in a poem
the dwarf trees of Baffin Island

JOHN CLARE

Song

Swamps of wild rush-beds, and sloughs' squashy traces,
  Grounds of rough fallows with thistle and weed,
Flats and low valleys of kingcups and daisies,
  Sweetest of subjects are ye for my reed:
Ye commons left free in the rude rags of nature,
  Ye brown heaths beclothed in furze as ye be,
My wild eye in rapture adores every feature,
  Ye are dear as this heart in my bosom to me.

O native endearments! I would not forsake ye,
  I would not forsake ye for sweetest of scenes;
For sweetest of gardens that nature could make me,
  I would not forsake ye, dear valleys and greens:
Tho' nature ne'er dropt ye a cloud-resting mountain,
  Nor waterfalls tumble their music so free;
Had nature denied ye a bush, tree, or fountain,
  Ye still had been lov'd as an Eden by me.

And long, my dear valleys, long, long may ye flourish,
  Though rush-beds and thistles make most of your pride;
May showers never fail the green's daisies to nourish,
  Nor suns dry the fountain that rills by its side.
Your skies may be gloomy, and misty your mornings,
  Your flat swampy valleys unwholesome may be;
Still, refuse of nature, without her adornings
  Ye are dear as this heart in my bosom to me.

ANONYMOUS

from Sir Gawain and the Green Knight

30

Now rides this renk thurgh the ryalme of Logres,
Sir Gauan, on Godes halve, thagh hym no gomen thoght.
Oft leudles alone he lenges on nyghtes,
Ther he fonde noght hym byfore the fare that he lyked.
Hade he no fere bot his fole bi frythes and dounes,
Ne no gome bot God bi gate wyth to karp,
Til that he neghed ful neghe into the Northe Wales.
Alle the iles of Anglesay on lyft half he haldes,
And fares over the fordes by the forlondes,
Over at the Holy Hede, til he hade eft bonk
In the wyldrenesse of Wyrale – wonde ther bot lyte
That auther God other gome wyth goud hert lovied.
And ay he fraayned, as he ferde, at frekes that he met,
If thay hade herde any karp of a knyght grene,
In any grounde theraboute, of the grene chapel;
And al nykked hym wyth nay, that never in her lyve
Thay seye never no segge that was of suche hwes
      of grene.
   The knyght tok gates straunge
   In mony a bonk unbene;
   His cher ful oft con chaunge,
   That chapel er he myght sene.

[Gawain's Journey North]

30

Now through the realm of England he rides and rides.
Sir Gawain, a servant of God, on his grim quest,
passing many a long night unloved and alone,
foraging to eat, finding little to call food,
with no friend but his horse through forests and hills
and no one to listen but the Almighty Lord.
He wanders his way near to the north of Wales.
Away to his left are the Anglesey Isles.
He keeps to the coast, fording each watercourse,
crossing at Holy Head and coming ashore
in the wilds of the Wirral, whose wayward people
both God and good-hearted men have given up on.
And he cautiously asks those that he comes across
whether or not, in this neck of the woods,
they tittle-tattle of a green knight or green temple.
No, they say, never. Never in all their lives.
They know of neither a knight or a chapel
        so strange.
    He trails through bleak terrain.
    His mood and manner change
    at every twist and turn
    towards that chosen church.

Mony klyf he overclambe in contrayes straunge,
Fer floten fro his frendes fremedly he rydes.
At uche warthe other water ther the wyye passed
He fonde a foo hym byfore, bot ferly hit were,
And that so foule and so felle that feght hym byhode.
So mony mervayl bi mount ther the mon fyndes,
Hit were to tore for to telle of the tenthe dole.
Sumwhyle wyth wormes he werres, and with wolves als,
Sumwhyle wyth wodwos that woned in the knarres,
Bothe wyth bulles and beres, and bores otherquyle,
And etaynes that hym anelede of the heghe felle.
Nade he ben dughty and dryye, and dryghtyn had served,
Douteles he hade ben ded and dreped ful ofte,
For werre wrathed hym not so much, that wynter was wors,
When the colde cler water fro the cloudes schadde,
And fres er hit falle myght to the fale erthe.
Ner slayn wyth the slete he sleped in his yrnes
Mo nyghtes then innoghe in naked rokkes,
Ther as claterande fro the crest the colde borne rennes,
And henged heghe over his hede in hard ysse-ikkles.
Thus in peryl and payne and plytes ful harde
Bi contray caryes this knyght tyl Krystmasse even,
       al one.
    The knyght wel that tyde
    To Mary made his mone,
    That ho hym red to ryde,
    And wysse hym to sum wone.

31

In a strange region he scales many steep slopes;
riding far from his friends he cuts a lonely figure.
Wherever he bridges or wades through a waterway
ill-fortune brings him face to face with a foe
so foul or fierce he is bound to use force.
So momentous are his travels among the mountains
to tell just a tenth of it would be a tall order.
Here he wrestles with snakes and snarling wolves,
here he tangles with trolls that lurk in the crags,
or battles with bulls and bears and the odd wild boar.
Giants are hard on his heels over the high ground.
Had he not been defiant, dutiful and devout,
by now that man would be nothing but dead meat.
And the wars were one thing, but winter was worse:
clouds shed their cargo of crystallized rain
which froze as it fell to the frost-glazed earth.
Numb to his marrow, he slept in his metal suit,
bivouacked in the blackness amongst bare rocks
where melt-water crashed from the snow-capped peaks
and high overhead hung chandeliers of ice.
So in peril and pain Sir Gawain progressed,
criss-crossing the countryside until Christmas
     Eve. Then
  at that time of tiding,
  he prayed to highest heaven.
  Let Mother Mary guide him
  towards some house or haven.

Translated by Simon Armitage

JAMES THOMSON

from The Seasons

Then spring the living herbs, profusely wild,
O'er all the deep-green earth, beyond the power
Of botanist to number up their tribes:
Whether he steals along the lonely dale
In silent search; or through the forest, rank
With what the dull incurious weeds account,
Bursts his blind way; or climbs the mountain-rock,
Fired by the nodding verdure of its brow,
With such a liberal hand has Nature flung
Their seeds abroad, blown them about in winds,
Innumerous mixed them with the nursing mould,
The moistening current, and prolific rain.
　　But who their virtues can declare? who pierce
With vision pure into these secret stores
Of health and life and joy? the food of man
While yet he lived in innocence, and told
A length of golden years, unfleshed in blood,
A stranger to the savage arts of life,
Death, rapine, carnage, surfeit, and disease –
The lord and not the tyrant of the world.
　　The first fresh dawn then waked the gladdened race
Of uncorrupted man, nor blushed to see
The sluggard sleep beneath its sacred beam;
For their light slumbers gently fumed away,
And up they rose as vigorous as the sun,
Or to the culture of the willing glebe,
Or to the cheerful tendance of the flock.
Meantime the song went round; and dance and sport,
Wisdom and friendly talk successive stole

Their hours away; while in the rosy vale
Love breathed his infant sighs, from anguish free,
And full replete with bliss – save the sweet pain
That, inly thrilling, but exalts it more.
Nor yet injurious act nor surly deed
Was known among these happy sons of heaven;
For reason and benevolence were law.
Harmonious Nature too looked smiling on.
Clear shone the skies, cooled with eternal gales,
And balmy spirit all. The youthful sun
Shot his best rays, and still the gracious clouds
Dropped fatness down; as o'er the swelling mead
The herds and flocks commixing played secure.
This when, emergent from the gloomy wood,
The glaring lion saw, his horrid heart
Was meekened, and he joined his sullen joy.
For music held the whole in perfect peace:
Soft sighed the flute; the tender voice was heard,
Warbling the varied heart; the woodlands round
Applied their quire; and winds and waters flowed
In consonance. Such were those prime of days.

WILLIAM CARLOS WILLIAMS

from Spring and All

I

By the road to the contagious hospital
under the surge of the blue
mottled clouds driven from the
northeast – a cold wind. Beyond, the
waste of broad, muddy fields
brown with dried weeds, standing and fallen

patches of standing water
the scattering of tall trees

All along the road the reddish
purplish, forked, upstanding, twiggy
stuff of bushes and small trees
with dead, brown leaves under them
leafless vines –

Lifeless in appearance, sluggish
dazed spring approaches –

They enter the new world naked,
cold, uncertain of all
save that they enter. All about them
the cold, familiar wind –

Now the grass, tomorrow
the stiff curl of wildcarrot leaf

One by one objects are defined –
It quickens: clarity, outline of leaf

But now the stark dignity of
entrance – Still, the profound change
has come upon them: rooted, they
grip down and begin to awaken

II

Pink confused with white
flowers and flowers reversed
take and spill the shaded flame
darting it back
into the lamp's horn

petals aslant darkened with mauve

red where in whorls
petal lays its glow upon petal
round flamegreen throats

petals radiant with transpiercing light
contending
                     above

the leaves
reaching up their modest green
from the pot's rim

and there, wholly dark, the pot
gay with rough moss.

ROBIN ROBERTSON

Primavera

for Cait

The brimstone is back
in the woken hills of Tuscany,
passing the word
from speedwell to violet
wood anemone to celandine.
I could walk to you now
with Spring just ahead of me,
north over flat ground
at two miles an hour,
the sap moving with me,
under the rising
grass of the field
like a dragged magnet,
the lights of the flowers
coming on in waves
as I walked with the budburst
and the flushing of trees.
If I started now,
I could bring you the Spring
for your birthday.

MAURICE RIORDAN

The January Birds

The birds in Nunhead Cemetery begin
Before I've flicked a switch, turned on the gas.
There must be some advantage to the light

I tell myself, viewing my slackened chin
Mirrored in the rain-dark window glass,
While from the graveyard's trees, the birds begin.

An image from a dream survives the night,
Some dreck my head refuses to encompass.
There must be some advantage to the light.

You are you I mouth to my shadow skin,
Though you are me, assuming weight and mass –
While from the graveyard's trees, the birds begin:

Thrush, blackbird, finch – then rooks take fright
At a skip-truck and protest, cawing *en masse.*
There must be some advantage to the light

Or birds would need the gift of second sight
To sing *Another year will come to pass!*
The birds in Nunhead Cemetery begin,
There must be some advantage to the light.

GARY SNYDER

Two Fawns That Didn't See the Light This Spring

A friend in a tipi in the
Northern Rockies went out
hunting white tail with a
.22 and creeped up on a few
day-bedded, sleeping, shot
what he thought was a buck.
'It was a doe, and she was
carrying a fawn.'
He cured the meat without
salt; sliced it following the
grain.

A friend in the Northern Sierra
hit a doe with her car. It
walked out calmly in the lights,
'And when we butchered her
there was a fawn – about so long –
so tiny – but all formed and right.
It had spots. And the little
hooves were soft and white.'

TED HUGHES

October Salmon

He's lying in poor water, a yard or so depth of poor safety,
Maybe only two feet under the no-protection of an
    outleaning small oak,
Half under a tangle of brambles.

After his two thousand miles, he rests,
Breathing in that lap of easy current
In his graveyard pool.

About six pounds weight,
Four years old at most, and hardly a winter at sea –
But already a veteran,
Already a death-patched hero. So quickly it's over!

So briefly he roamed the gallery of marvels!
Such sweet months, so richly embroidered into earth's
    beauty-dress,
Her life-robe –
Now worn out with her tirelessness, her insatiable quest,
Hangs in the flow, a frayed scarf –

An autumnal pod of his flower,
The mere hull of his prime, shrunk at shoulder and flank,

With the sea-going Aurora Borealis
Of his April power –
The primrose and violet of that first upfling in the estuary –
Ripened to muddy dregs,
The river reclaiming his sea-metals.

In the October light
He hangs there, patched with leper-cloths.

Death has already dressed him
In her clownish regimentals, her badges and decorations,
Mapping the completion of his service,
His face a ghoul-mask, a dinosaur of senility, and his whole
    body
A fungoid anemone of canker –

Can the caress of water ease him?
The flow will not let up for a minute.

What a change! from that covenant of polar light
To this shroud in a gutter!
What a death-in-life – to be his own spectre!
His living body become death's puppet,
Dolled by death in her crude paints and drapes
He haunts his own staring vigil
And suffers the subjection, and the dumbness,
And the humiliation of the role!

And that is how it is,
That is what is going on there, under the scrubby oak tree,
    hour after hour,
That is what the splendour of the sea has come down to,
And the eye of ravenous joy – king of infinite liberty
In the flashing expanse, the bloom of sea-life,

On the surge-ride of energy, weightless,
Body simply the armature of energy
In that earliest sea-freedom, the savage amazement of life,
The salt mouthful of actual existence
With strength like light –

Yet this was always with him. This was inscribed in his egg.
This chamber of horrors is also home.
He was probably hatched in this very pool.

And this was the only mother he ever had, this uneasy channel
   of minnows
Under the mill-wall, with bicycle wheels, car tyres, bottles
And sunk sheets of corrugated iron.
People walking their dogs trail their evening shadows across
   him.
If boys see him they will try to kill him.

All this, too, is stitched into the torn richness,
The epic poise
That holds him so steady in his wounds, so loyal to his doom,
   so patient
In the machinery of heaven.

EDWARD THOMAS

'Out in the Dark'

Out in the dark over the snow
The fallow fawns invisible go
With the fallow doe;
And the winds blow
Fast as the stars are slow.

Stealthily the dark haunts round
And, when the lamp goes, without sound
At a swifter bound
Than the swiftest hound,
Arrives, and all else is drowned;

And I and star and wind and deer,
Are in the dark together, – near,
Yet far, – and fear
Drums on my ear
In that sage company drear.

How weak and little is the light,
All the universe of sight,
Love and delight,
Before the might,
If you love it not, of night.

KATHLEEN JAMIE

Crossing the Loch

Remember how we rowed toward the cottage
on the sickle-shaped bay,
that one night after the pub
loosed us through its swinging doors
and we pushed across the shingle
till water lipped the sides
as though the loch mouthed 'boat'?

I forget who rowed. Our jokes hushed.
The oars' splash, creak, and the spill
of the loch reached long into the night.
Out in the race I was scared:
the cold shawl of breeze,
and hunched hills; what the water held
of deadheads, ticking nuclear hulls.

Who rowed, and who kept their peace?
Who hauled salt-air and stars
deep into their lungs, were not reassured;
and who first noticed the loch's
phosphorescence, so, like a twittering nest
washed from the rushes, an astonished
small boat of saints, we watched water shine
on our fingers and oars,
the magic dart of our bow wave?

It was surely foolhardy, such a broad loch, a tide,
but we live – and even have children
to women and men we had yet to meet
that night we set out, calling our own
the sky and salt-water, wounded hills
dark-starred by blaeberries, the glimmering anklets
we wore in the shallows
as we shipped oars and jumped,
to draw the boat safe, high at the cottage shore.

ALLISON FUNK

Ephemeroptera

for my brother David

Blizzard. Smoke. Interstellar
dust. Even you, an entomologist,
turn to metaphor,

awed by their emergence
over water. So thick
at times you cover your face

to keep from breathing them in.
Pale evening dun,
morning spinner.

How many dawns ago,
numberless dusks?
Call it

what astronomers do –
that past whose light
is just now reaching us:

look-back time. Yours
and mine – our own becoming,
born of the milky ways

of love. Fragile once
as the earliest larva,
brother, instar.

And later – in a house looking out
into a woods of tulip poplar,
rhododendron, down over train tracks

to a creek named Red Clay
where, in another eon,
fish swam before men

put out the lights of mayflies
smaller than the thumb
of the boy with a net

you were then.
Twenty-nine-o-one,
our address as children blurring

with the thousand-some species
of *Ephemeroptera,*
with prehistory, fossil time,

the millions of years mayflies
thrived in Permian streams,
Triassic, Jurassic,

feeding on infinitesimal diatoms
before vanishing
from our fouled creek.

It's another century
and we've been gone
from home as long as it's taken

them to return one by one
to their underworld
of silt and mud.

Some clinging to stones
in swift currents, others
hiding in gaps. With oar-like gills

the unbleached nymph
rows for dear oxygen,
spending years in between-time

molting over and over
again, as often as we've left
a self behind –

all for as much
as a single evening
when this wisp

growing not toward death
but into something
like the passions that consume us,

filamentous, breaks the water's surface
with crumpled wings
and, fast as a sleight of hand,

changes shape a final time
to become the luminous, meteoric
imago,

in whose likeness
may I recognize in what passes
what lasts.

ROBERT FROST

To a Moth Seen in Winter

Here's first a gloveless hand warm from my pocket,
A perch and resting place 'twixt wood and wood,
Bright-black-eyed silvery creature, brushed with brown,
The wings not folded in repose, but spread.
(Who would you be, I wonder, by those marks
If I had moths to friend as I have flowers?)
And now pray tell what lured you with false hope
To make the venture of eternity
And seek the love of kind in wintertime?
But stay and hear me out. I surely think
You make a labor of flight for one so airy,
Spending yourself too much in self-support.
Nor will you find love either, nor love you.
And what I pity in you is something human,
The old incurable untimeliness,
Only begetter of all ills that are.
But go. You are right. My pity cannot help.
Go till you wet your pinions and are quenched.
You must be made more simply wise than I
To know the hand I stretch impulsively
Across the gulf of well-nigh everything
May reach to you, but cannot touch your fate.
I cannot touch your life, much less can save,
Who am tasked to save my own a little while.

ALEXANDER POPE

from An Essay on Man

Far as Creation's ample range extends,
The scale of sensual, mental pow'rs ascends:
Mark how it mounts, to Man's imperial race,
From the green myriads in the peopled grass:
What modes of sight betwixt each wide extreme,
The mole's dim curtain, and the lynx's beam:
Of smell, the headlong lioness between,
And hound sagacious on the tainted green:
Of hearing, from the life that fills the flood,
To that which warbles thro' the vernal wood:
The spider's touch, how exquisitely fine!
Feels at each thread, and lives along the line:
In the nice bee, what sense so subtly true
From pois'nous herbs extracts the healing dew:
How Instinct varies in the grov'ling swine,
Compar'd, half-reas'ning elephant, with thine:
'Twixt that, and Reason, what a nice barrier;
For ever sep'rate, yet for ever near!
Remembrance and Reflection how ally'd;
What thin partitions Sense from Thought divide:
And Middle natures, how they long to join,
Yet never pass th'insuperable line!
Without this just gradation, could they be
Subjected these to those, or all to thee?
The pow'rs of all subdu'd by thee alone,
Is not thy Reason all these pow'rs in one?

See, thro' this air, this ocean, and this earth,
All matter quick, and bursting into birth.
Above, how high progressive life may go!
Around, how wide! how deep extend below!
Vast chain of being, which from God began,
Natures aethereal, human, angel, man,
Beast, bird, fish, insect! what no eye can see,
No glass can reach! from Infinite to thee,
From thee to Nothing! – On superior pow'rs
Were we to press, inferior might on ours:
Or in the full creation leave a void,
Where, one step broken, the great scale's destroy'd:
From Nature's chain whatever link you strike,
Tenth or ten thousandth, breaks the chain alike.

ROBERT BURNS

To a Mouse, on Turning Her Up in Her Nest, with the Plough, November, 1785

Wee, sleeket, cowran, tim'rous *beastie*,
O, what a panic's in thy breastie!
Thou need na start awa sae hasty,
   Wi' bickering brattle!
I wad be laith to rin an' chase thee,
   Wi' murd'ring *pattle*!

I'm truly sorry Man's dominion
Has broken Nature's social union,
An' justifies that ill opinion,
   Which makes thee startle,
At me, thy poor, earth-born companion,
   An' *fellow-mortal*!

I doubt na, whyles, but thou may *thieve*;
What then? poor beastie, thou maun live!
A *daimen-icker* in a *thrave*
   'S a sma' request:
I'll get a blessin wi' the lave,
   An' never miss't!

Thy wee-bit *housie*, too, in ruin!
It's silly wa's the win's are strewin!
An' naething, now, to big a new ane,
   O' foggage green!
An' bleak *December's winds* ensuin,
   Baith snell an' keen!

Thou saw the fields laid bare an' wast,
An' weary *Winter* comin fast,
An' cozie here, beneath the blast,
   Thou thought to dwell,
Till crash! the cruel *coulter* past
   Out thro' thy cell.

That wee-bit heap o' leaves an' stibble,
Has cost thee monie a weary nibble!
Now thou 's turn'd out, for a' thy trouble,
   But house or hald,
To thole the Winter's *sleety dribble*,
   An' *cranreuch* cauld!

But Mousie, thou art no thy-lane,
In proving *foresight* may be vain:
The best laid schemes o' *Mice* an' *Men*,
   Gang aft agley,
An' lea'e us nought but grief an' pain,
   For promis'd joy!

Still, thou art blest, compar'd wi' *me*!
The *present* only toucheth thee:
But Och! I *backward* cast my e'e,
   On prospects drear!
An' *forward*, tho' I canna *see*,
   I *guess* an' *fear*!

sleeket glossy; *bickering brattle* scurrying haste; *laith* loath; *pattle* spade;
whyles at times; *daimen-icker* odd ear of corn; *thrave* two stooks; *lave*
remainder; *big* build; *foggage* grass; *snell* bitter; *But* without; *hald*
refuge; *thole* endure; *cranreuch* frost; *no thy-lane* not alone; *agley* away

JOHN CLARE

The Badger

The badger grunting on his woodland track
With shaggy hide and sharp nose scrowed with black
Roots in the bushes and the woods and makes
A great hugh burrow in the ferns and brakes
With nose on ground he runs a awkward pace
And anything will beat him in the race
The shepherds dog will run him to his den
Followed and hooted by the dogs and men
The woodman when the hunting comes about
Go round at night to stop the foxes out
And hurrying through the bushes ferns and brakes
Nor sees the many holes the badger makes
And often through the bushes to the chin
Breaks the old holes and tumbles headlong in

When midnight comes a host of dogs and men
Go out and track the badger to his den
And put a sack within the hole and lye
Till the old grunting badger passes bye
He comes and hears they let the strongest loose
The old fox hears the noise and drops the goose
The poacher shoots and hurrys from the cry
And the old hare half wounded buzzes bye
They get a forked stick to bear him down
And clapt the dogs and bore him to the town
And bait him all the day with many dogs
And laugh and shout and fright the scampering hogs
He runs along and bites at all he meets
They shout and hollo down the noisey streets

He turns about to face the loud uproar
And drives the rebels to their very doors
The frequent stone is hurled where ere they go
When badgers fight and every ones a foe
The dogs are clapt and urged to join the fray
The badger turns and drives them all away
Though scarcely half as big dimute and small
He fights with dogs for hours and beats them all
The heavy mastiff savage in the fray
Lies down and licks his feet and turns away
The bull dog knows his match and waxes cold
The badger grins and never leaves his hold
He drives the crowd and follows at their heels
And bites them through the drunkard swears and reels

The frighted women takes the boys away
The blackguard laughs and hurrys on the fray
He trys to reach the woods a awkward race
But sticks and cudgels quickly stop the chace
He turns agen and drives the noisey crowd
And beats the many dogs in noises loud
He drives away and beats them every one
And then they loose them all and set them on
He falls as dead and kicked by boys and men
Then starts and grins and drives the crowd agen
Till kicked and torn and beaten out he lies
And leaves his hold and cackles groans and dies

Some keep a baited badger tame as hog
And tame him till he follows like the dog
They urge him on like dogs and show fair play
He beats and scarcely wounded goes away
Lapt up as if asleep he scorns to fly
And siezes any dog that ventures nigh
Clapt like a dog he never bites the men

But worrys dogs and hurrys to his den
They let him out and turn a barrow down
And there he fights the pack of all the town
He licks the patting hand and trys to play
And never trys to bite or run away
And runs away from noise in hollow trees
Burnt by the boys to get a swarm of bees

MARGARET CAVENDISH, DUCHESS OF NEWCASTLE

The Hunting of the Hare

Betwixt two ridges of ploughed land lay Wat,
Pressing his body close to earth lay squat.
His nose upon his two forefeet close lies,
Glaring obliquely with his great grey eyes.
His head he always sets against the wind:
If turn his tail, his hairs blow up behind,
Which he too cold will grow; but he is wise,
And keeps his coat still down, so warm he lies.
Thus resting all the day, till sun doth set,
Then riseth up, his relief for to get,
Walking about until the sun doth rise;
Then back returns, down in his form he lies.
At last poor Wat was found, as there he lay,
By huntsmen with their dogs which came that way.
Seeing, gets up, and fast begins to run,
Hoping some ways the cruel dogs to shun.
But they by nature have so quick a scent
That by their nose they trace what way he went;
And with their deep, wide mouths set forth a cry
Which answered was by echoes in the sky.
Then Wat was struck with terror and with fear,
Thinks every shadow still the dogs they were;
And running out some distance from the noise
To hide himself, his thoughts he new employs.
Under a clod of earth in sandpit wide,
Poor Wat sat close, hoping himself to hide.
There long he had not sat but straight his ears
The winding horns and crying dogs he hears:
Starting with fear up leaps, then doth he run,

And with such speed, the ground scarce treads upon.
Into a great thick wood he straightway gets,
Where underneath a broken bough he sits;
At every leaf that with the wind did shake
Did bring such terror, made his heart to ache.
That place he left; to champian plains he went,
Winding about, for to deceive their scent,
And while they snuffling were, to find his track,
Poor Wat, being weary, his swift pace did slack.
On his two hinder legs for ease did sit:
His forefeet rubbed his face from dust and sweat.
Licking his feet, he wiped his ears so clean
That none could tell that Wat had hunted been.
But casting round about his fair great eyes,
The hounds in full career he near him spies;
To Wat it was so terrible a sight,
Fear gave him wings, and made his body light.
Though weary was before, by running long,
Yet now his breath he never felt more strong.
Like those that dying are, think health returns,
When 'tis but a faint blast which life out burns.
For spirits seek to guard the heart about,
Striving with death; but death doth quench them out.
Thus they so fast came on, with such loud cries,
That he no hopes hath left, nor help espies.
With that the winds did pity poor Wat's case,
And with their breath the scent blew from the place.
Then every nose is busily employed,
And every nostril is set open wide;
And every head doth seek a several way
To find what grass or track the scent on lay.
Thus quick industry, that is not slack,
Is like to witchery, brings lost things back.
For though the wind had tied the scent up close,
A busy dog thrust in his snuffling nose,

And drew it out, with it did foremost run;
Then horns blew loud, for the rest to follow on.
The great slow hounds, their throats did set a base,
The fleet swift hounds as tenors next in place;
The little beagles they a treble sing,
And through the air their voice a round did ring;
Which made a consort as they ran along:
If they but words could speak, might sing a song:
The horns kept time, the hunters shout for joy,
And valiant seem, poor Wat for to destroy.
Spurring their horses to a full career,
Swim rivers deep, leap ditches without fear;
Endanger life and limbs, so fast will ride,
Only to see how patiently Wat died.
For why, the dogs so near his heels did get
That they their sharp teeth in his breech did set.
Then tumbling down, did fall with weeping eyes,
Gives up his ghost, and thus poor Wat he dies.
Men hooping loud such acclamations make
As if the devil they did prisoner take,
When they do but a shiftless creature kill,
To hunt, there needs no valiant soldier's skill.
But man doth think that exercise and toil,
To keep their health, is best, which makes most spoil;
Thinking that food and nourishment so good,
And appetite, that feeds on flesh and blood.
When they do lions, wolves, bears, tigers see
To kill poor sheep, straight say, they cruel be;
But for themselves all creatures think too few,
For luxury, wish God would make them new.
As if that God made creatures for man's meat,
And gave them life and sense, for man to eat;
Or else for sport, or recreation's sake,
Destroy those lives that God saw good to make;
Making their stomachs graves, which full they fill

With murthered bodies that in sport they kill.
Yet man doth think himself so gentle, mild,
When of all creatures he's most cruel wild;
And is so proud, thinks only he shall live,
That God a godlike nature did him give,
And that all creatures for his sake alone
Was made for him to tyrannize upon.

grow cause to become; *still* ever; *relief* food; *form* lair; *close* secret;
champian unenclosed; *breech* rump; *shiftless* helpless

WILLIAM COWPER

Epitaph on a Hare

Here lies, whom hound did ne'er pursue,
   Nor swifter greyhound follow,
Whose foot ne'er tainted morning dew,
   Nor ear heard huntsman's halloo;

Old Tiney, surliest of his kind,
   Who, nursed with tender care,
And to domestic bounds confined,
   Was still a wild Jack hare.

Though duly from my hand he took
   His pittance every night,
He did it with a jealous look,
   And, when he could, would bite.

His diet was of wheaten bread,
   And milk, and oats, and straw;
Thistles, or lettuces instead,
   With sand to scour his maw.

On twigs of hawthorn he regaled,
   On pippins' russet peel,
And, when his juicy salads fail'd,
   Sliced carrot pleased him well.

A Turkey carpet was his lawn,
   Whereon he loved to bound,
To skip and gambol like a fawn,
   And swing his rump around.

His frisking was at evening hours,
  For then he lost his fear,
But most before approaching showers,
  Or when a storm drew near.

Eight years and five round-rolling moons
  He thus saw steal away,
Dozing out all his idle noons,
  And every night at play.

I kept him for his humour's sake,
  For he would oft beguile
My heart of thoughts that made it ache,
  And force me to a smile.

But now beneath his walnut shade
  He finds his long last home,
And waits, in snug concealment laid,
  Till gentler Puss shall come.

He, still more aged, feels the shocks
  From which no care can save,
And, partner once of Tiney's box,
  Must soon partake his grave.

JAMES DICKEY

The Heaven of Animals

Here they are. The soft eyes open.
If they have lived in a wood
It is a wood.
If they have lived on plains
It is grass rolling
Under their feet forever.

Having no souls, they have come,
Anyway, beyond their knowing.
Their instincts wholly bloom
And they rise.
The soft eyes open.

To match them, the landscape flowers,
Outdoing, desperately
Outdoing what is required:
The richest wood,
The deepest field.

For some of these,
It could not be the place
It is, without blood.
These hunt, as they have done,
But with claws and teeth grown perfect,

More deadly than they can believe.
They stalk more silently,
And crouch on the limbs of trees,
And their descent
Upon the bright backs of their prey

May take years
In a sovereign floating of joy.
And those that are hunted
Know this as their life,
Their reward: to walk

Under such trees in full knowledge
Of what is in glory above them,
And to feel no fear,
But acceptance, compliance.
Fulfilling themselves without pain

At the cycle's center,
They tremble, they walk
Under the tree,
They fall, they are torn,
They rise, they walk again.

LES MURRAY

Pigs

Us all on sore cement was we.
Not warmed then with glares. Not glutting mush
under that pole the lightning's tied to.
No farrow-shit in milk to make us randy.
Us back in cool god-shit. We ate crisp.
We nosed up good rank in the tunnelled bush.
Us all fuckers then. And Big, huh? Tusked
the balls-biting dog and gutsed him wet.
Us shoved down the soft cement of rivers.
Us snored the earth hollow, filled farrow, grunted.
Never stopped growing. We sloughed, we soughed
and balked no weird till the high ridgebacks was us
with weight-buried hooves. Or bristly, with milk.
Us never knowed like slitting nor hose-biff then.
Not the terrible sheet-cutting screams up ahead.
The burnt water kicking. This gone-already feeling
here in no place with our heads on upside down.

JOHN DRYDEN

from Of the Pythagorean Philosophy

'And therefore I conclude; whatever lies
In earth, or flits in air, or fills the skies,
All suffer change, and we, that are of soul
And body mixed, are members of the whole.
Then, when our sires, or grandsires, shall forsake
The forms of men, and brutal figures take,
Thus housed, securely let their spirits rest,
Nor violate thy father in the beast.
Thy friend, thy brother, any of thy kin,
Is none of these, yet there's a man within:
O spare to make a Thyestean meal,
To enclose his body, and his soul expel.
  'Ill customs by degrees to habits rise,
Ill habits soon become exalted vice:
What more advance can mortals make in sin
So near perfection, who with blood begin?
Deaf to the calf that lies beneath the knife,
Looks up, and from her butcher begs her life;
Deaf to the harmless kid, that ere he dies
All methods to procure thy mercy tries,
And imitates in vain thy children's cries.
Where will he stop, who feeds with household bread,
Then eats the poultry which before he fed?
Let plough thy steers; that when they lose their breath
To nature, not to thee, they may impute their death.
Let goats for food their loaded udders lend,
And sheep from winter-cold thy sides defend;
But neither springes, nets, nor snares employ,
And be no more ingenious to destroy.

Free as in air, let birds on earth remain,
Nor let insidious glue their wings constrain;
Nor opening hounds the trembling stag affright,
Nor purple feathers intercept his flight:
Nor hooks concealed in baits for fish prepare,
Nor lines to heave them twinkling up in air.
   'Take not away the life you cannot give;
For all things have an equal right to live.
Kill noxious creatures, where 'tis sin to save;
This only just prerogative we have:
But nourish life with vegetable food,
And shun the sacrilegious taste of blood.'

PAUL MULDOON

Glaucus

It went without saying that a king of Corinth
should keep his prize fillies out of the fray
and, rather than have them enmesh
themselves in horse-toils, horse-tattle,

set them up, each on a plinth,
and fillet their manes with knots and nosegays
and feed them the choicest human flesh
to give them a taste for battle.

It went without saying that after he lost control
of his chariot-team at Pelias, and made a hames
of setting them all square,

Glaucus was still on such a roll
it was lost on him that the high point of the games
was his being eaten now by his own mares.

THOMAS HARDY

Wagtail and Baby

A baby watched a ford, whereto
   A wagtail came for drinking;
A blaring bull went wading through,
   The wagtail showed no shrinking.

A stallion splashed his way across,
   The birdie nearly sinking;
He gave his plumes a twitch and toss,
   And held his own unblinking.

Next saw the baby round the spot
   A mongrel slowly slinking:
The wagtail gazed, but faltered not
   In dip and sip and prinking.

A perfect gentleman then neared;
   The wagtail, in a winking,
With terror rose and disappeared;
   The baby fell a-thinking.

ANDREW MARVELL

The Mower against Gardens

Luxurious man, to bring his vice in use,
  Did after him the world seduce,
And from the fields the flowers and plants allure,
  Where nature was most plain and pure.
He first enclosed within the garden's square
  A dead and standing pool of air,
And a more luscious earth for them did knead,
  Which stupefied them while it fed.
The pink grew then as double as his mind;
  The nutriment did change the kind.
With strange perfúmes he did the roses taint;
  And flowers themselves were taught to paint.
The tulip, white, did for complexion seek,
  And learned to interline its cheek:
Its onion root they then so high did hold,
  That one was for a meadow sold.
Another world was searched, through oceans new,
  To find the Marvel of Peru.
And yet these rarities might be allowed
  To man, that sovereign thing and proud,
Had he not dealt between the bark and tree,
  Forbidden mixtures there to see.
No plant now knew the stock from which it came;
  He grafts upon the wild the tame:
That the uncertain and adulterate fruit
  Might put the palate in dispute.
His green seraglio has its eunuchs too,
  Lest any tyrant him outdo.

And in the cherry he does nature vex,
    To procreate without a sex.
'Tis all enforced, the fountain and the grot,
    While the sweet fields do lie forgot;
Where willing nature does to all dispense
    A wild and fragrant innocence:
And fauns and fairies do the meadows till,
    More by their presence than their skill.
Their statues, polished by some ancient hand,
    May to adorn the gardens stand:
But howsoe'er the figures do excel,
    The gods themselves with us do dwell.

MICHAEL SYMMONS ROBERTS

To John Donne

Unlike an area of land, when you patent a gene,
you are enclosing a part of me, the shared landscape.
Sir John Sulston

Now, as your mistress strips for bed,
her body is already mapped,
its ancient names a cracked code.

That new found land is paced out,
sized up, written down as hope
or prophecy, probability or doubt.

Her charts are held on laptops,
mastered by medics, laid bare.
Her peaks and gorges, fell slopes,

oceans, woodlands, stars,
this atlas of her is no mystic book,
it is a textbook of disease.

The sun turns dust to smoke,
and picks out, as it sets,
a path your hands might take

– your roving hands – she lets
them roam, though she's no landowner.
By law, her breast's

curve has a patent, so you know
that bankers — tired of gold —
have bought a piece of her and you.

You call her your America — too right.
Her wilderness, those prairies
have been carved up into real estate,

ranches ringed with barbed wire,
lights and guns. KEEP OUT
OUR DOGS EAT TRESPASSERS.

Do you care? Does she? What
can it matter at this fleet May dusk,
as you seek each other out,

and her body's secret name is much
like yours, and yours is so close
to the crab apple and silver birch

which interweave with collar doves
and greenfinches, akin to grass
which drapes in blossom as the light dies.

Let your hands, and hers, lead us
in love's mass trespass, let your lips,
and hers, claim back with whispers

the co-ordinates of bodies: TTA,
GAG, TGT, CCC, ATC, TGT *(this is,
yes, a litany)* CTG, GAG, TTG …

BEN JONSON

To Penshurst

Thou art not, Penshurst, built to envious show,
  Of touch or marble; nor canst boast a row
Of polished pillars, or a roof of gold;
  Thou hast no lantern whereof tales are told,
Or stair, or courts; but stand'st an ancient pile,
  And, these grudged at, art reverenced the while.
Thou joy'st in better marks, of soil, of air,
  Of wood, of water; therein thou are fair.
Thou hast thy walks for health, as well as sport;
  Thy mount, to which the dryads do resort,
Where Pan and Bacchus their high feasts have made,
  Beneath the broad beech and the chestnut shade;
That taller tree, which of a nut was set
  At his great birth where all the Muses met.
There in the writhèd bark are cut the names
  Of many a sylvan, taken with his flames;
And thence the ruddy satyrs oft provoke
  The lighter fauns to reach thy Lady's Oak.
Thy copse too, named of Gamage, thou hast there,
  That never fails to serve thee seasoned deer
When thou wouldst feast or exercise thy friends.
  The lower land, that to the river bends,
Thy sheep, thy bullocks, kine, and calves do feed;
  The middle grounds thy mares and horses breed.
Each bank doth yield thee conies; and the tops,
  Fertile of wood, Ashore and Sidney's copse,
To crown thy open table, doth provide
  The purpled pheasant with the speckled side;

The painted partridge lies in every field,
  And for thy mess is willing to be killed.
And if the high swollen Medway fail thy dish,
  Thou hast thy ponds, that pay thee tribute fish:
Fat agèd carps that run into thy net,
  And pikes, now weary their own kind to eat,
As loath the second draught or cast to stay,
  Officiously at first themselves betray;
Bright eels that emulate them, and leap on land
  Before the fisher, or into his hand.
Then hath thy orchard fruit, thy garden flowers,
  Fresh as the air, and new as are the hours.
The early cherry, with the later plum,
  Fig, grape, and quince, each in his time doth come;
The blushing apricot and woolly peach
  Hang on thy walls, that every child may reach.
And though thy walls be of the country stone,
  They're reared with no man's ruin, no man's groan;
There's none that dwell about them wish them down;
  But all come in, the farmer and the clown,
And no one empty-handed, to salute
  Thy lord and lady, though they have no suit.
Some bring a capon, some a rural cake,
  Some nuts, some apples; some that think they make
The better cheeses bring them, or else send
  By their ripe daughters, whom they would commend
This way to husbands, and whose baskets bear
  An emblem of themselves in plum or pear.
But what can this (more than express their love)
  Add to thy free provisions, far above
The need of such? whose liberal board doth flow
  With all that hospitality doth know;
Whence comes no guest but is allowed to eat,
  Without his fear, and of thy lord's own meat;

Where the same beer and bread, and selfsame wine,
   That is his lordship's shall be also mine,
And I not fain to sit (as some this day
   At great men's tables), and yet dine away.
Here no man tells my cups; nor, standing by,
   A waiter doth my gluttony envy,
But gives me what I call, and lets me eat;
   He knows below he shall find plenty of meat.
Thy tables hoard not up for the next day;
   Nor, when I take my lodging, need I pray
For fire, or lights, or livery; all is there,
   As if thou then wert mine, or I reigned here:
There's nothing I can wish, for which I stay.
   That found King James when, hunting late this way
With his brave son, the Prince, they saw thy fires
   Shine bright on every hearth, as the desires
Of thy Penates had been set on flame
   To entertain them; or the country came
With all their zeal to warm their welcome here.
   What (great I will not say, but) sudden cheer
Didst thou then make 'em! and what praise was heaped
   On thy good lady then, who therein reaped
The just reward of her high housewifery;
   To have her linen, plate, and all things nigh,
When she was far; and not a room but dressed
   As if it had expected such a guest!
These, Penshurst, are thy praise, and yet not all.
   Thy lady's noble, fruitful, chaste withal.
His children thy great lord may call his own,
   A fortune in this age but rarely known.
They are, and have been, taught religion; thence
   Their gentler spirits have sucked innocence.
Each morn and even they are taught to pray,
   With the whole household, and may, every day,

Read in their virtuous parents' noble parts
    The mysteries of manners, arms, and arts.
Now, Penshurst, they that will proportion thee
    With other edifices, when they see
Those proud, ambitious heaps, and nothing else,
    May say, their lords have built, but thy lord dwells.

MARIANNE MOORE

The Steeple-Jack

Dürer would have seen a reason for living
    in a town like this, with eight stranded whales
to look at; with the sweet sea air coming into your house
on a fine day, from water etched
    with waves as formal as the scales
on a fish.

One by one in two's and three's, the seagulls keep
    flying back and forth over the town clock,
or sailing around the lighthouse without moving their wings –
rising steadily with a slight
    quiver of the body – or flock
mewing where

a sea the purple of the peacock's neck is
    paled to greenish azure as Dürer changed
the pine green of the Tyrol to peacock blue and guinea
gray. You can see a twenty-five-
    pound lobster; and fish nets arranged
to dry. The

whirlwind fife-and-drum of the storm bends the salt
    marsh grass, disturbs stars in the sky and the
star on the steeple; it is a privilege to see so
much confusion. Disguised by what
    might seem the opposite, the sea-
side flowers and

trees are favored by the fog so that you have
     the tropics at first hand: the trumpet-vine,
fox-glove, giant snap-dragon, a salpiglossis that has
spots and stripes; morning-glories, gourds,
     or moon-vines trained on fishing-twine
at the back door;

cat-tails, flags, blueberries and spiderwort,
     striped grass, lichens, sunflowers, asters, daisies –
yellow and crab-claw ragged sailors with green bracts – toad-plant,
petunias, ferns; pink lilies, blue
     ones, tigers; poppies; black sweet-peas.
The climate

is not right for the banyan, frangipani, or
     jack-fruit trees; or for exotic serpent
life. Ring lizard and snake-skin for the foot, if you see fit;
but here they've cats, not cobras, to
     keep down the rats. The diffident
little newt

with white pin-dots on black horizontal spaced-
     out bands lives here; yet there is nothing that
ambition can buy or take away. The college student
named Ambrose sits on the hillside
     with his not-native books and hat
and sees boats

at sea progress white and rigid as if in
     a groove. Liking an elegance of which
the source is not bravado, he knows by heart the antique
sugar-bowl shaped summer-house of
     interlacing slats, and the pitch
of the church

spire, not true, from which a man in scarlet lets
    down a rope as a spider spins a thread;
he might be part of a novel, but on the sidewalk a
sign says C. J. Poole, Steeple-Jack,
    in black and white; and one in red
and white says

Danger. The church portico has four fluted
    columns, each a single piece of stone, made
modester by white-wash. This would be a fit haven for
waifs, children, animals, prisoners,
    and presidents who have repaid
sin-driven

senators by not thinking about them. The
    place has a school-house, a post-office in a
store, fish-houses, hen-houses, a three-masted schooner on
the stocks. The hero, the student,
    the steeple-jack, each in his way,
is at home.

It could not be dangerous to be living
    in a town like this, of simple people,
who have a steeple-jack placing danger-signs by the church
while he is gilding the solid-
    pointed star, which on a steeple
stands for hope.

ERIC PANKEY

Metaphor

To capture the morning
    along the washed-out town road
above a slope too steep to grow crops
    he shoveled up this tangle
        of weeds and grasses –

    each separate, clustered:
        feathery shoots of yarrow,
dandelion florets closed tight above
    their jagged damp leaves, cocksfoot,
        spare spikes of heath rush

    and fleshy plantain.
        He carried it home before
the dew dried, before the green mass grown
    heavy with itself wilted.
        The sod in his hands

    was wet and ragged
        with white tubers and nerve-like
roots. The dirt sifted through his hands
    fell in a trail behind him.
        Posed at eye-level

    on a shelf above
        his table the square of earth
grew richer as he painted –
    creeping Charlie, meadow grass,
        clear for the first time

as the light, which was
    by now water and color,
dried still and permanent on paper.
    Springtime held in check, steadfast.
        A cool wash of green.

A study, he called
    it later. An exercise
toward some greater painting. Perhaps
    the wild growth among the rocks
        of Calvary hill,

or beneath the head
    of a waking guard surprised
by light from a tomb that bright morning
    when spring arrived forever.
        In this old story

about a painting,
    in this long meditation
there is another, unknown story
    about the young apprentice
        who mumbled and bitched

as again he swept
    the floor after his master
tracked in the red-clay soil, the straw
    thrown down outside the doorstep.
        When the boy stopped work

long enough to say
    he had had enough, he quit,
the artist did not look up, did not
    take his eyes off the green clump
        losing its luster.

The boy cared nothing
   for a mess of weeds, for years
of calculating the pure proportion
  of head to hand to body,
    the raw stink of oil.

Although his trained hands
   were skilled enough to copy
Christ's passion, a body in torture ...,
  he cared nothing for beauty.
    He wanted to be

a soldier, wanted
   to feel the taut right angle
of a bow-string as he released it
  shimmer into music.
    He wanted to go

to the Promised Land.
   So he gave up sweeping
and walked out into the clearing day.
  He walked the rutted roadway
    pocked with black puddles

south away from town.
   The old man could have his weeds,
he thought, stopping by the embankment
  from which the sod had been cut.
    It looked like what it

was – a scar of mud,
   not a grave's first shovelful
torn away. He did not believe in
  metaphor enough to see
    it as that, a grave.

LINDA GREGERSON

Elegant

Dewpoint and a level field. Or slick
    of agar,

  microscope,
       the embryonic roundworm and
an open mind. The world so rarely

       lets us in, let's
       praise

  the lucky vista when it does.
     We knew,
said my tutor, that death was a part of it, think

  of the webbing that's eaten away in
     order
    that you may have fingers. We

      didn't know – how to put this? – before

  we mapped our soil-borne roundworm, *c.*

    for *Caenor-* (filth) *hab-*
  ditus (one who dwells there) with

its thousand and ninety invariant
       cells of which
    131 and always
  the same

and always in a particular sequence are programmed
for extinction,
                    we had no idea how close
                    to the heart of it death
                                        must be.
        At first

                a sort of cratered field, or
                                    granulated – see it? – both

        the raised parts and con–
                            cavities, the sculpting
                                            light,

    and then a sort of swelling (it's a corpse now) then
                        engulfment (that's
                    the sister cell) and then

                                the disappearance (you'll
            remember how the lipids 'lose their place').

    And on our chart an *x* where would

                be daughter cells, 'a fate
                like any other.' It's

a lie, of course, the light

        and shadow so disposed, a
                            friendly
    lie, *as if* as in a play: of

                something less congenial to the seeing

            eye, the microscope

makes shadow and
our question gains some traction and the world,

though not
just yet and not
so seamlessly, makes sense.

Proprietary sequencing? Don't
break my heart.

We thought at first a camera
would be just the thing, the thing itself in real
time caught for anyone

to stop
and start, but that

was to ignore how much the camera
misses, how what we call seeing

in an ever-changing depth

of field while (twofold,
threefold, turning on its axis, still

unhatched) our worm

performs its complex cleavages and differentiations
is already
to have balanced on the scales

of thought. What
answered, what
the optics (see *Nomarski*) really
needed on the other end

was homely as the worm: a pencil,

paper, one man preternat–
                urally good at this, and
         thirteen hours,
      a little more, from founder cell to hatching (let's say

coffee, lots). And found
         he had transcribed there? Found

      that death was not an afterthought. The genome
        is a river too. And simpler, far

                  more elegant, to

keep the single system and discard the extra cells
            it spawns. So *apo*–

(*Gk.*, away from) *ptosis* (fall), as leaves

         preserve the tree by learning
     to relinquish it. A river
        of intelligence runs through us, could
the part we do on purpose do

      less harm. One version
of the lesson is its usefulness, the kindred
        genes that help us break the circuit

     of malignancy, we name them for what happens when
       they fail.
       But use is not

the whole of it. *He wants*, said my father (and this
    of one he loved), *to live*

forever, so I knew it was contemptible (had loved
forever). Death

is not an afterthought nor

(mother of beauty) will death
undone assist us, we
are made of it, are cognate (mother) to the worm, a worthy

daily labor and this thread
of in-the-cells remembering make it so.

C. elegans

JOHN MILTON

from **Paradise Lost**
[The Prospect of Eden]

So on he fares, and to the border comes
Of Eden, where delicious Paradise,
Now nearer, crowns with her enclosure green,
As with a rural mound, the champain head
Of a steep wilderness, whose hairy sides
With thicket overgrown, grotesque and wild,
Access denied; and overhead up-grew
Insuperable highth of loftiest shade,
Cedar, and pine, and fir, and branching palm,
A sylvan scene, and, as the ranks ascend
Shade above shade, a woody theatre
Of stateliest view. Yet higher than their tops
The verdurous wall of Paradise up-sprung;
Which to our general sire gave prospect large
Into his nether empire neighbouring round.
And higher than that wall a circling row
Of goodliest trees, loaden with fairest fruit,
Blossoms and fruits at once of golden hue,
Appeared, with gay enamelled colours mixed;
On which the sun more glad impressed his beams
Than in fair evening cloud, or humid bow,
When God hath showered the earth: so lovely seemed
That landskip. And of pure now purer air
Meets his approach, and to the heart inspires
Vernal delight and joy, able to drive
All sadness but despair. Now gentle gales,
Fanning their odoriferous wings, dispense
Native perfumes, and whisper whence they stole

Those balmy spoils. As, when to them who sail
Beyond the Cape of Hope, and now are past
Mozambic, off at sea north-east winds blow
Sabean odours from the spicy shore
Of Araby the Blest, with such delay
Well pleased they slack their course, and many a league
Cheered with the grateful smell old Ocean smiles;
So entertained those odorous sweets the Fiend
Who came their bane, though with them better pleased
Than Asmodëus with the fishy fume
That drove him, though enamoured, from the spouse
Of Tobit's son, and with a vengeance sent
From Media post to Egypt, there fast bound.
   Now to the ascent of that steep savage hill
Satan had journeyed on, pensive and slow;
But further way found none; so thick entwined,
As one continued brake, the undergrowth
Of shrubs and tangling bushes had perplexed
All path of man or beast that passed that way.
One gate there only was, and that looked east
On the other side. Which when the Arch-Felon saw,
Due entrance he disdained, and, in contempt,
At one slight bound high overleaped all bound
Of hill or highest wall, and sheer within
Lights on his feet.

WILLIAM WORDSWORTH

Nutting

_____ It seems a day
(I speak of one from many singled out)
One of those heavenly days that cannot die;
When, in the eagerness of boyish hope,
I left our cottage-threshold, sallying forth
With a huge wallet o'er my shoulders slung,
A nutting-crook in hand; and turned my steps
Toward some far-distant wood, a Figure quaint,
Tricked out in proud disguise of cast-off weeds
Which for that service had been husbanded,
By exhortation of my frugal Dame –
Motley accoutrement, of power to smile
At thorns, and brakes, and brambles, – and, in truth,
More ragged than need was! O'er pathless rocks,
Through beds of matted fern, and tangled thickets,
Forcing my way, I came to one dear nook
Unvisited, where not a broken bough
Drooped with its withered leaves, ungracious sign
Of devastation; but the hazels rose
Tall and erect, with tempting clusters hung,
A virgin scene! – A little while I stood,
Breathing with such suppression of the heart
As joy delights in; and, with wise restraint
Voluptuous, fearless of a rival, eyed
The banquet; – or beneath the trees I sate
Among the flowers, and with the flowers I played;
A temper known to those who, after long
And weary expectation, have been blest
With sudden happiness beyond all hope.

Perhaps it was a bower beneath whose leaves
The violets of five seasons re-appear
And fade, unseen by any human eye;
Where fairy water-breaks do murmur on
For ever; and I saw the sparkling foam,
And – with my cheek on one of those green stones
That, fleeced with moss, under the shady trees,
Lay round me, scattered like a flock of sheep –
I heard the murmur and the murmuring sound,
In that sweet mood when pleasure loves to pay
Tribute to ease; and, of its joy secure,
The heart luxuriates with indifferent things,
Wasting its kindliness on stocks and stones,
And on the vacant air. Then up I rose,
And dragged to earth both branch and bough, with crash
And merciless ravage: and the shady nook
Of hazels, and the green and mossy bower,
Deformed and sullied, patiently gave up
Their quiet being: and, unless I now
Confound my present feelings with the past,
Ere from the mutilated bower I turned
Exulting, rich beyond the wealth of kings,
I felt a sense of pain when I beheld
The silent trees, and saw the intruding sky. –
Then, dearest Maiden, move along these shades
In gentleness of heart; with gentle hand
Touch – for there is a spirit in the woods.

THEODORE ROETHKE

Moss-Gathering

To loosen with all ten fingers held wide and limber
And lift up a patch, dark-green, the kind for lining cemetry
  baskets,
Thick and cushiony, like an old-fashioned doormat,
The crumbling small hollow sticks on the underside mixed with
  roots,
And wintergreen berries and leaves still stuck to the top, –
That was moss-gathering.
But something always went out of me when I dug loose those
  carpets
Of green, or plunged to my elbows in the spongy yellowish
  moss of the marshes:
And afterwards I always felt mean, jogging back over the
  logging road,
As if I had broken the natural order of things in that
  swampland;
Disturbed some rhythm, old and of vast importance,
By pulling off flesh from the living planet;
As if I had committed, against the whole scheme of life, a
  desecration.

ALGERNON CHARLES SWINBURNE

The Sundew

A little marsh-plant, yellow green,
And pricked at lip with tender red.
Tread close, and either way you tread
Some faint black water jets between
Lest you should bruise the curious head.

A live thing maybe; who shall know?
The summer knows and suffers it;
For the cool moss is thick and sweet
Each side, and saves the blossom so
That it lives out the long June heat.

The deep scent of the heather burns
About it; breathless though it be,
Bow down and worship; more than we
Is the least flower whose life returns,
Least weed renascent in the sea.

We are vexed and cumbered in earth's sight
With wants, with many memories;
These see their mother what she is,
Glad-growing, till August leave more bright
The apple-coloured cranberries.

Wind blows and bleaches the strong grass,
Blown all one way to shelter it
From temple of strayed kine, with feet
Felt heavier than the moorhen was,
Strayed up past patches of wild wheat.

You call it sundew: how it grows,
If with its colour it have breath,
If life taste sweet to it, if death
Pain its soft petal, no man knows:
Man has no sight or sense that saith.

My sundew, grown of gentle days,
In these green miles the spring begun
Thy growth ere April had half done
With the soft secret of her ways
Or June made ready for the sun.

O red-lipped mouth of marsh-flower,
I have a secret halved with thee.
The name that is love's name to me
Thou knowest, and the face of her
Who is my festival to see.

The hard sun, as thy petals knew,
Coloured the heavy moss-water:
Thou wert not worth green midsummer
Nor fit to live to August blue,
O sundew, not remembering her.

SIDNEY LANIER

The Marshes of Glynn

Glooms of the live-oaks, beautiful-braided and woven
With intricate shades of the vines that myriad-cloven
  Clamber the forks of the multiform boughs, –
      Emerald twilights, –
      Virginal shy lights,
Wrought of the leaves to allure to the whisper of vows,
When lovers pace timidly down through the green colonnades
  Of the dim sweet woods, of the dear dark woods,
      Of the heavenly woods and glades,
  That run to the radiant marginal sand-beach within
      The wide sea-marshes of Glynn; –

  Beautiful glooms, soft dusks in the noon-day fire, –
  Wildwood privacies, closets of lone desire,
Chamber from chamber parted with wavering arras of leaves, –
Cells for the passionate pleasure of prayer to the soul that grieves,
  Pure with a sense of the passing of saints through the wood,
  Cool for the dutiful weighing of ill with good; –
O braided dusks of the oak and woven shades of the vine,
While the riotous noon-day sun of the June-day long did shine,
Ye held me fast in your heart and I held you fast in mine;
  But now when the noon is no more, and riot is rest,
  And the sun is a-wait at the ponderous gate of the West,
    And the slant yellow beam down the wood-aisle doth seem
    Like a lane into heaven that leads from a dream, –
Ay, now, when my soul all day hath drunken the soul of the oak,
And my heart is at ease from men, and the wearisome sound of
                         the stroke

Of the scythe of time and the trowel of trade is low,
And belief overmasters doubt, and I know that I know,
And my spirit is grown to a lordly great compass within,
That the length and the breadth and the sweep of the
marshes of Glynn
Will work me no fear like the fear they have wrought me of
yore
When length was fatigue, and when breadth was but
bitterness sore,
And when terror and shrinking and dreary unnamable pain
Drew over me out of the merciless miles of the plain, –
Oh, now, unafraid, I am fain to face
The vast sweet visage of space.
To the edge of the wood I am drawn, I am drawn,
Where the gray beach glimmering runs, as a belt of the dawn,
For a mete and a mark
To the forest-dark: –
So:
Affable live-oak, leaning low, –
Thus – with your favor – soft, with a reverend hand,
(Not lightly touching your person, Lord of the land!)
Bending your beauty aside, with a step I stand
On the firm-packed sand,
Free
By a world of marsh that borders a world of sea.
Sinuous southward and sinuous northward the shimmering band
Of the sand-beach fastens the fringe of the marsh to the folds
of the land.
Inward and outward to northward and southward the
beachlines linger and curl
As a silver-wrought garment that clings to and follows the
firm sweet limbs of a girl.
Vanishing, swerving, evermore curving again into sight,

Softly the sand-beach wavers away to a dim gray looping of
                                                          light.
And what if behind me to westward the wall of the woods
                                                    stands high?
The world lies east: how ample, the marsh and the sea and
                                                       the sky!
A league and a league of marsh-grass, waist-high, broad in
                                                      the blade,
Green, and all of a height, and unflecked with a light or a
                                                        shade,
   Stretch leisurely off, in a pleasant plain,
   To the terminal blue of the main.

  Oh, what is abroad in the marsh and the terminal sea?
    Somehow my soul seems suddenly free
From the weighing of fate and the sad discussion of sin,
  By the length and the breadth and the sweep of the marshes
                                                      of Glynn,
Ye marshes, how candid and simple and nothing-withholding
                                                     and free
Ye publish yourselves to the sky and offer yourselves to the sea!
Tolerant plains, that suffer the sea and the rains and the sun,
Ye spread and span like the catholic man who hath mightily won
  God out of knowledge and good out of infinite pain
  And sight out of blindness and purity out of a stain.

As the marsh-hen secretly builds on the watery sod,
Behold I will build me a nest on the greatness of God:
I will fly in the greatness of God as the marsh-hen flies
In the freedom that fills all the space 'twixt the marsh and
                                                      the skies:
By so many roots as the marsh-grass sends in the sod
I will heartily lay me a-hold on the greatness of God:

Oh, like to the greatness of God is the greatness within
  The range of the marshes, the liberal marshes of Glynn.
And the sea lends large, as the marsh: lo, out of his plenty the sea
  Pours fast: full soon the time of the flood-tide must be:
    Look how the grace of the sea doth go
  About and about through the intricate channels that flow
        Here and there,
        Everywhere,
Till his waters have flooded the uttermost creeks and the
                                low-lying lanes,
  And the marsh is meshed with a million veins,
  That like as with rosy and silvery essences flow
    In the rose-and-silver evening glow.
        Farewell, my lord Sun!
  The creeks overflow: a thousand rivulets run
  'Twixt the roots of the sod; the blades of the marsh-grass stir;
Passeth a hurrying sound of wings that westward whirr;
Passeth, and all is still; and the currents cease to run;
    And the sea and the marsh are one.

    How still the plains of the waters be!
    The tide is in his ecstasy.
    The tide is at his highest height:
        And it is night.

  And now from the Vast of the Lord will the waters of sleep
      Roll in on the souls of men,
    But who will reveal to our waking ken
    The forms that swim and the shapes that creep
      Under the waters of sleep?
And I would I could know what swimmeth below when the
                                tide comes in
  On the length and the breadth of the marvellous marshes of
                                Glynn.

A. R. AMMONS

Corsons Inlet

I went for a walk over the dunes again this morning
to the sea,
then turned right along
   the surf
                  rounded a naked headland
                  and returned

   along the inlet shore:

it was muggy sunny, the wind from the sea steady and high,
crisp in the running sand,
     some breakthroughs of sun
   but after a bit

continuous overcast:

the walk liberating, I was released from forms,
from the perpendiculars,
     straight lines, blocks, boxes, binds
of thought
into the hues, shadings, rises, flowing bends and blends
       of sight:

                 I allow myself eddies of meaning:
yield to a direction of significance
running
like a stream through the geography of my work:
    you can find
in my sayings

swerves of action
like the inlet's cutting edge:
there are dunes of motion,
organizations of grass, white sandy paths of remembrance
in the overall wandering of mirroring mind:

but Overall is beyond me: is the sum of these events
I cannot draw, the ledger I cannot keep, the accounting
beyond the account:

in nature there are few sharp lines: there are areas of
primrose
more or less dispersed;
disorderly orders of bayberry; between the rows
of dunes,
irregular swamps of reeds,
though not reeds alone, but grass, bayberry, yarrow, all ...
predominantly reeds:

I have reached no conclusions, have erected no boundaries,
shutting out and shutting in, separating inside
from outside: I have
drawn no lines:
as

manifold events of sand
change the dune's shape that will not be the same shape
tomorrow,

so I am willing to go along, to accept
the becoming
thought, to stake off no beginnings or ends, establish
no walls:

by transitions the land falls from grassy dunes to creek
to undercreek: but there are no lines, though
        change in that transition is clear
        as any sharpness: but 'sharpness' spread out,
allowed to occur over a wider range
than mental lines can keep:

the moon was full last night: today, low tide was low:
black shoals of mussels exposed to the risk
of air
and, earlier, of sun,
waved in and out with the waterline, waterline inexact,
caught always in the event of change:
        a young mottled gull stood free on the shoals
        and ate
to vomiting: another gull, squawking possession, cracked a crab,
picked out the entrails, swallowed the soft-shelled legs, a ruddy
turnstone running in to snatch leftover bits:

risk is full: every living thing in
siege: the demand is life, to keep life: the small
white blacklegged egret, how beautiful, quietly stalks and spears
        the shallows, darts to shore
            to stab – what? I couldn't
        see against the black mudflats – a frightened
        fiddler crab?

        the news to my left over the dunes and
reeds and bayberry clumps was
        fall: thousands of tree swallows
        gathering for flight:
        an order held
        in constant change: a congregation
rich with entropy: nevertheless, separable, noticeable
        as one event,

not chaos: preparations for
flight from winter,
cheet, cheet, cheet, cheet, wings rifling the green clumps,
beaks
at the bayberries
   a perception full of wind, flight, curve,
   sound:
   the possibility of rule as the sum of rulelessness:
the 'field' of action
with moving, incalculable center:

in the smaller view, order tight with shape:
blue tiny flowers on a leafless weed: carapace of crab:
snail shell:
         pulsations of order
         in the bellies of minnows: orders swallowed,
broken down, transferred through membranes
to strengthen larger orders: but in the large view, no
lines or changeless shapes: the working in and out, together
       and against, of millions of events: this,
           so that I make
           no form of
           formlessness:

orders as summaries, as outcomes of actions override
or in some way result, not predictably (seeing me gain
the top of a dune,
the swallows
could take flight – some other fields of bayberry
       could enter fall
       berryless) and there is serenity:

no arranged terror: no forcing of image, plan,
or thought:
no propaganda, no humbling of reality to precept:

terror pervades but is not arranged, all possibilities
of escape open: no route shut, except in
    the sudden loss of all routes:

        I see narrow orders, limited tightness, but will
not run to that easy victory:
        still around the looser, wider forces work:
        I will try
    to fasten into order enlarging grasps of disorder, widening
scope, but enjoying the freedom that
Scope eludes my grasp, that there is no finality of vision,
that I have perceived nothing completely,
        that tomorrow a new walk is a new walk.

MARY OLIVER

Heron Rises from the Dark, Summer Pond

So heavy
is the long-necked, long-bodied heron,
always it is a surprise
when her smoke-colored wings

open
and she turns
from the thick water,
from the black sticks

of the summer pond,
and slowly
rises into the air
and is gone.

Then, not for the first or the last time,
I take the deep breath
of happiness, and I think
how unlikely it is

that death is a hole in the ground,
how improbable
that ascension is not possible,
though everything seems so inert, so nailed

back into itself —
the muskrat and his lumpy lodge,
the turtle,
the fallen gate.

And especially it is wonderful
that the summers are long
and the ponds so dark and so many,
and therefore it isn't a miracle

but the common thing,
this decision,
this trailing of the long legs in the water,
this opening up of the heavy body

into a new life: see how the sudden
gray-blue sheets of her wings
strive toward the wind; see how the clasp of nothing
takes her in.

Waterbuffalo

Waterbuffalo walk, they walk as if in sleep to the water,
Hip-gloss of light rolls on each black ball-joint and belly,
   bulk-head,
shiny as something melting.

Shiny as melting
these slow-strung beasts recline, recline
into the water, their knees give –

bodies turning they go down like a wall like slow death
they half-coil onto one side,
sigh, and fold
into the water,
paying themselves out
through the oilskin surface, and begin to glide.

The water moves, brown and muscular.
Mosquito larvae wring themselves along,
and curds of sickness stir in the mud.

Far out in the cooler water the buffalo rest, silent,
each a live head set on that table,
with a rack of horn, warm at the root, risen ringed and scaly
   from the skull;
throat held out flat, and chin on the water,
their dark blocks of bodies turned to weightless light.

D. H. LAWRENCE

Snake

A snake came to my water-trough
On a hot, hot day, and I in pyjamas for the heat,
To drink there.

In the deep, strange-scented shade of the great dark carob-tree
I came down the steps with my pitcher
And must wait, must stand and wait, for there he was at the
    trough before me.

He reached down from a fissure in the earth-wall in the gloom
And trailed his yellow-brown slackness soft-bellied down, over
    the edge of the stone trough
And rested his throat upon the stone bottom,
And where the water had dripped from the tap, in a small
    clearness,
He sipped with his straight mouth,
Softly drank through his straight gums, into his slack long
    body,
Silently.

Someone was before me at my water-trough,
And I, like a second comer, waiting.

He lifted his head from his drinking, as cattle do,
And looked at me vaguely, as drinking cattle do,
And flickered his two-forked tongue from his lips, and mused
    a moment,
And stooped and drank a little more,

Being earth-brown, earth-golden from the burning bowels of
    the earth
On the day of Sicilian July, with Etna smoking.

The voice of my education said to me
He must be killed,
For in Sicily the black, black snakes are innocent, the gold are
    venomous.

And voices in me said, If you were a man
You would take a stick and break him now, and finish him off.

But must I confess how I liked him,
How glad I was he had come like a guest in quiet, to drink at
    my water-trough
And depart peaceful, pacified, and thankless,
Into the burning bowels of this earth?

Was it cowardice, that I dared not kill him?
Was it perversity, that I longed to talk to him?
Was it humility, to feel so honoured?
I felt so honoured.

And yet those voices:
If you were not afraid, you would kill him!

And truly I was afraid, I was most afraid,
But even so, honoured still more
That he should seek my hospitality
From out the dark door of the secret earth.

He drank enough
And lifted his head, dreamily, as one who has drunken,
And flickered his tongue like a forked night on the air, so
    black,

Seeming to lick his lips,
And looked around like a god, unseeing, into the air,
And slowly turned his head,
And slowly, very slowly, as if thrice adream,
Proceeded to draw his slow length curving round
And climb again the broken bank of my wall-face.

And as he put his head into that dreadful hole,
And as he slowly drew up, snake-easing his shoulders, and
    entered farther,
A sort of horror, a sort of protest against his withdrawing into
    that horrid black hole,
Deliberately going into the blackness, and slowly drawing
    himself after,
Overcame me now his back was turned.

I looked round, I put down my pitcher,
I picked up a clumsy log
And threw it at the water-trough with a clatter.

I think it did not hit him,
But suddenly that part of him that was left behind convulsed
    in undignified haste,
Writhed like lightning, and was gone
Into the black hole, the earth-lipped fissure in the wall-front.
At which, in the intense still noon, I stared with fascination.

And immediately I regretted it.
I thought how paltry, how vulgar, what a mean act!
I despised myself and the voices of my accursed human
    education.

And I thought of the albatross,
And I wished he would come back, my snake.

For he seemed to me again like a king,
Like a king in exile, uncrowned in the underworld,
Now due to be crowned again.

And so, I missed my chance with one of the lords
Of life.
And I have something to expiate;
A pettiness.

ROBERT FROST

Two Look at Two

Love and forgetting might have carried them
A little further up the mountainside
With night so near, but not much further up.
They must have halted soon in any case
With thoughts of the path back, how rough it was
With rock and washout, and unsafe in darkness;
When they were halted by a tumbled wall
With barbed-wire binding. They stood facing this,
Spending what onward impulse they still had
In one last look the way they must not go,
On up the failing path, where, if a stone
Or earthslide moved at night, it moved itself;
No footstep moved it. 'This is all,' they sighed,
'Good-night to woods.' But not so; there was more.
A doe from round a spruce stood looking at them
Across the wall, as near the wall as they.
She saw them in their field, they her in hers.
The difficulty of seeing what stood still,
Like some up-ended boulder split in two,
Was in her clouded eyes: they saw no fear there.
She seemed to think that, two thus, they were safe.
Then, as if they were something that, though strange,
She could not trouble her mind with too long,
She sighed and passed unscared along the wall.
'This, then, is all. What more is there to ask?'
But no, not yet. A snort to bid them wait.
A buck from round the spruce stood looking at them
Across the wall, as near the wall as they.
This was an antlered buck of lusty nostril,

Not the same doe come back into her place.
He viewed them quizzically with jerks of head,
As if to ask, 'Why don't you make some motion?
Or give some sign of life? Because you can't.
I doubt if you're as living as you look.'
Thus till he had them almost feeling dared
To stretch a proffering hand – and a spell-breaking.
Then he too passed unscared along the wall.
Two had seen two, whichever side you spoke from.
'This *must* be all.' It was all. Still they stood,
A great wave from it going over them,
As if the earth in one unlooked-for favor
Had made them certain earth returned their love.

JAMES LASDUN

A Peeled Wand

September clearness, insects
glinting on the far shore;
bullfrogs, red-wing blackbirds –
the dial-tone of summer –
bubbling up through the warm evening air ...
Out on the water a snapper
snags a V of ripples
towards us – no, not a snapper;
we slow to a halt
as whatever it is circles closer
till we see him, suddenly clear in the water,
the curves of his half-submerged brow
bulging on the surface
like the smooth bulges on tree trunks
loggers call cat-face flaws;
forelegs working beneath him,
leisurely, as though walking on air;
and now, closer still,
in the bluestone-bottomed shallows,
he rises, holding aloft
the deep, dripping boat of his head,
calmly scanning the bankside thickets,
and with a shake, a little shiver
to mark the exchange of elements,
steps from the water,
lumbering right across our path,
and with two audible snips,
snips through an alder sapling
(the young bark still glossy brown)

in a salad of its own leaves
and shoulders it back to the shallows,
where with the same leisured unconcern
for anything but his own ease,
he strips off and chews, one by one,
every twig and leaf,
washing each mouthful down
with a sip of our clear silver water
then glides off
for a between-courses swim
halfway across the reservoir,
paddle-tail wafting him
through a reflected mountain ...
It's winter now,
snow like wool, as the psalm says, mists like ashes.
I think of him out there again, taking his ease
in the late summer evening sweetness
of sumac and goldenrod,
swimming unhurriedly back
for the tender bark of the sapling,
(the best part, we had to suppose)
turning the stick with his hands, nibbling
the tight skin clear from the greenwood –
all but a few tough inches at the thick end
left like a leather-bound hilt or handle –
then with a last look around him
at the lilac-edged ring of mountains
and the sky like a jeweler's tray
with a sun and an opal moon
and two or three choice stars,
heading off back where he came from,
fanning a fishtail wake on the water
and leaving behind him the peeled wand:
I have it here in my hand.

NORMAN MACCAIG

Toad

Stop looking like a purse. How could a purse
squeeze under the rickety door and sit,
full of satisfaction, in a man's house?

You clamber towards me on your four corners –
right hand, left foot, left hand, right foot.

I love you for being a toad,
for crawling like a Japanese wrestler,
and for not being frightened.

I put you in my purse hand, not shutting it,
and set you down outside directly under
every star.

A jewel in your head? Toad,
you've put one in mine,
a tiny radiance in a dark place.

JOSEPH CAMPBELL

Ad Limina

The ewes and lambs, loving the far hillplaces,
Cropping by choice the succulent tops of heather,
Drinking the pure water of cloudborn lochlands,
Resting under erratics fostered with Abel –
Come to my haggard gate, my very doorstep.

The birds of freest will and strongest wingbeat,
Sad curlew, garrulous stonechat, hawk and coaltit,
Haunting lone bog or scalp or broken ruin,
Poising the rough thrust of air's excesses –
Come to my haggard gate, my very doorstep.

The trout in the river, below the hanging marllot,
Swift, with ancestral fear of hook and shadow,
The elvers of cold drain and slough, remembering
The warm tangles of Caribbee and Sargasso –
Come to my haggard gate, my very doorstep.

Even the stoats and rats, who know a possessor
Of the rare sixth sense, the bardic insight,
Match, and more, for their devilish perversions,
And the deer, shyest of shy at autumn rutting –
Come to my haggard gate, my very doorstep.

Am I not a lucky man, trusted, Franciscan,
That these spacious things, gentle or hostile,
Following God's urge, denying their nature,
Harbingers of high thoughts and fathers of poems –
Come to my haggard gate, my very doorstep.

WALT WHITMAN

from Song of Myself

I think I could turn and live with animals, they are so placid
    and self-contain'd,
I stand and look at them long and long.

They do not sweat and whine about their condition,
They do not lie awake in the dark and weep for their sins,
They do not make me sick discussing their duty to God,
Not one is dissatisfied, not one is demented with the mania of
    owning things,
Not one kneels to another, nor to his kind that lived
    thousands of years ago,
Not one is respectable or unhappy over the whole earth.

So they show their relations to me and I accept them,
They bring me tokens of myself, they evince them plainly in
    their possession.

I wonder where they get those tokens,
Did I pass that way huge times ago and negligently drop
    them?

Myself moving forward then and now and forever,
Gathering and showing more always and with velocity,
Infinite and omnigenous, and the like of these among them,
Not too exclusive toward the reachers of my remembrancers,
Picking out here one that I love, and now go with him on
    brotherly terms.

A gigantic beauty of a stallion, fresh and responsive to my
    caresses,
Head high in the forehead, wide between the ears,
Limbs glossy and supple, tail dusting the ground,
Eyes full of sparkling wickedness, ears finely cut, flexibly
    moving.

His nostrils dilate as my heels embrace him,
His well-built limbs tremble with pleasure as we race around
    and return.

I but use you a minute, then I resign you, stallion,
Why do I need your paces when I myself out-gallop them?
Even as I stand or sit passing faster than you.

W.S. MERWIN

Visitation

Two natives of the bare mountains   appear in the doorway
first I saw the dogs coming   far down the gold slope

the men shuffle and say hello   rimmed with sunlight
and ask if I've seen anything   up here all morning
winds of autumn are passing   over the uplands
migrations of shadows   crossing dry grass
clouds keep running the wall   of dark peaks to the south
ragged flocks trail   through the calling sky

but these had in mind   the animals
had I seen them at all   that made the hoofprints
or a sign of the hare   the quail or the partridge
no I tell them   and they nod and look away

how do I like it up here they ask
but they won't come in   they were just passing
don't mind the dogs they say   and they tell me
the name of where they come from   and step from the
   doorway

every year they say   it's harder to find them
the animals   even up here
and I say is that true   and they laugh

SIR PHILIP SIDNEY

from The Countess of Pembroke's Arcadia

Such manner time there was (what time I not)
When all this earth, this dam or mould of ours,
Was only woned with such as beasts begot;
Unknown as then were they that builden towers.
The cattle, wild or tame, in nature's bowers
  Might freely roam or rest, as seemed them;
  Man was not man their dwellings in to hem.

The beasts had sure some beastly policy;
For nothing can endure where order nis.
For once the lion by the lamb did lie;
The fearful hind the leopard did kiss;
Hurtless was tiger's paw and serpent's hiss.
  This think I well: the beasts with courage clad
  Like senators a harmless empire had.

At which, whether the others did repine
(For envy harb'reth most in feeblest hearts),
Or that they all to changing did incline
(As e'en in beasts their dams leave changing parts),
The multitude to Jove a suit imparts,
  With neighing, bleaing, braying, and barking,
  Roaring, and howling, for to have a king.

A king in language theirs they said they would
(For then their language was a perfect speech).
The birds likewise with chirps and pewing could,
Cackling and chatt'ring, that of Jove beseech.
Only the owl still warned them not to seech
  So hastily that which they would repent;
  But saw they would, and he to deserts went.

Jove wisely said (for wisdom wisely says):
'O beasts, take heed what you of me desire.
Rulers will think all things made them to please,
And soon forget the swink due to their hire.
But since you will, part of my heav'nly fire
  I will you lend; the rest yourselves must give,
  That it both seen and felt may with you live.'

Full glad they were, and took the naked sprite,
Which straight the earth yclothed in his clay.
The lion, heart; the ounce gave active might;
The horse, good shape; the sparrow, lust to play;
Nightingale, voice, enticing songs to say.
  Elephant gave a perfect memory;
  And parrot, ready tongue, that to apply.

The fox gave craft; the dog gave flattery;
Ass, patience; the mole, a working thought;
Eagle, high look; wolf, secret cruelty;
Monkey, sweet breath; the cow, her fair eyes brought;
The ermine, whitest skin spotted with naught;
  The sheep, mild-seeming face; climbing, the bear;
  The stag did give the harm-eschewing fear.

The hare her sleights; the cat his melancholy;
Ant, industry; and cony, skill to build;
Cranes, order; storks, to be appearing holy;
Chameleon, ease to change; duck, ease to yield;
Crocodile, tears which might be falsely spilled.
    Ape great thing gave, though he did mowing stand:
    The instrument of instruments, the hand.

Each other beast likewise his present brings;
And (but they drad their prince they oft should want)
They all consented were to give him wings.
And ay more awe towards him for to plant,
To their own work this privilege they grant:
    That from thenceforth to all eternity
    No beast should freely speak, but only he.

Thus man was made; thus man their lord became;
Who at the first, wanting or hiding pride,
He did to beasts' best use his cunning frame,
With water drink, herbs meat, and naked hide,
And fellow-like let his dominion slide,
    Not in his sayings saying 'I', but 'we';
    As if he meant his lordship common be.

But when his seat so rooted he had found
That they now skilled not how from him to wend,
Then gan in guiltless earth full many a wound,
Iron to seek, which gainst itself should bend
To tear the bowels that good corn should send.
    But yet the common dam none did bemoan,
    Because (though hurt) they never heard her groan.

Then gan he factions in the beasts to breed;
Where helping weaker sort, the nobler beasts
(As tigers, leopards, bears, and lions' seed)
Disdained with this, in deserts sought their rests;
Where famine ravin taught their hungry chests,
   That craftily he forced them to do ill;
   Which being done, he afterwards would kill

For murder done, which never erst was seen,
By those great beasts. As for the weakers' good,
He chose themselves his guarders for to been
Gainst those of might of whom in fear they stood,
As horse and dog; not great, but gentle blood.
   Blithe were the commons, cattle of the field,
   Tho when they saw their foen of greatness killed.

But they, or spent or made of slender might,
Then quickly did the meaner cattle find,
The great beams gone, the house on shoulders light;
For by and by the horse fair bits did bind;
The dog was in a collar taught his kind.
   As for the gentle birds, like case might rue
   When falcon they, and goshawk, saw in mew.

Worst fell to smallest birds, and meanest herd,
Who now his own, full like his own he used.
Yet first but wool, or feathers, off he teared;
And when they were well used to be abused,
For hungry throat their flesh with teeth he bruised;
   At length for glutton taste he did them kill;
   At last for sport their silly lives did spill.

But yet, O man, rage not beyond thy need;
Deem it no gloire to swell in tyranny.
Thou art of blood; joy not to make things bleed.
Thou fearest death; think they are loath to die.
A plaint of guiltless hurt doth pierce the sky.
   And you, poor beasts, in patience bide your hell,
   Or know your strengths, and then you shall do well.

Thus did I sing and pipe eight sullen hours
To sheep whom love, not knowledge, made to hear;
Now fancy's fits, now fortune's baleful stours.
But then I homeward called my lambkins dear;
For to my dimmed eyes began t'appear
   The night grown old, her black head waxen grey,
   Sure shepherd's sign that morn would soon fetch day.

ANONYMOUS

'The Robin and the Redbreast'

The robin and the redbreast,
  The robin and the wren,
If you take them out of their nest,
  Ye'll never thrive again.

The robin and the redbreast,
  The martin and the swallow;
If you touch one of their eggs,
  Ill luck is sure to follow.

PAUL FARLEY

An Ovaltine Tin in the Egg Collections at Tring

If, at the end of the day as they say, these eggs
tell a story set in negative space, then it's right
the tin I caught sight of stacked in a corner
should have its say, a battered by-product
brought in after a spring-clean or a clear-out;
I could play it over my knee, bash out a tune,
but prefer to let this one speak for itself,
emptied twice over, if you see what I mean,

shiny inside, metallic as the moon,
the outside meant for a world I don't understand
just as a blackbird's egg seems out of place
laid out on cotton wool, removed from leaf shadow
or nettle bed. Caskets for collections
of garden birds, I say speak for yourselves
and there's just a huge silence of course, although
the brand names call out, as they were designed to:

Craven A, Huntley & Palmers, Oxo,
Crawford's, Jacob's, Peak Freans' Assorted Creams,
Selesta fondants, Ogden's, Ovaltine ...
Some sing on while others ring hollow,
a half-remembered jingle from the undergrowth
that turns this tin into a kind of music box,
and when I push and seal the lid back on
there's a silence twice over, if you see what I mean.

GEOFFREY CHAUCER

from The Parliament of Fowls
[Catalogue of the Birds]

Whan I was come ayeyn into the place
That I of spak, that was so sote and grene,
Forth welk I tho myselven to solace.
Tho was I war wher that ther sat a queene
That, as of lyght the somer sonne shene
Passeth the sterre, right so over mesure
She fayrer was than any creature.

And in a launde, upon an hil of floures,
Was set this noble goddesse Nature.
Of braunches were here halles and here boures
Iwrought after here cast and here mesure;
Ne there nas foul that cometh of engendrure
That they ne were prest in here presence,
To take hire dom and yeve hire audyence.

For this was on seynt Valentynes day,
Whan every foul cometh there to chese his make,
Of every kynde that men thynke may,
And that so huge a noyse gan they make
That erthe, and eyr, and tre, and every lake
So ful was, that unethe was there space
For me to stonde, so ful was al the place.

sote sweet; *welk* walked; *sterre* stars; *over mesure* beyond measure; *launde*
glade; *here* her; *cast* design; *foul* bird; *engendrure* procreation; *prest* eagerly
ready; *take hire dom* receive her decision; *audyence* hearing; *chese his*
make choose its mate; *unethe* hardly

And right as Aleyn, in the Pleynt of Kynde,
Devyseth Nature of aray and face,
In swich aray men myghte hire there fynde.
This noble emperesse, ful of grace,
Bad every foul to take his owne place,
As they were woned alwey fro yer to yeere,
Seynt Valentynes day, to stonden theere.

That is to seyn, the foules of ravyne
Weere hyest set, and thanne the foules smale
That eten, as hem Nature wolde enclyne,
As worm or thyng of which I telle no tale;
And water-foul sat lowest in the dale;
But foul that lyveth by sed sat on the grene,
And that so fele that wonder was to sene.

There myghte men the royal egle fynde,
That with his sharpe lok perseth the sonne,
And othere egles of a lowere kynde,
Of whiche that clerkes wel devyse conne.
Ther was the tiraunt with his fetheres donne
And grey, I mene the goshauk, that doth pyne
To bryddes for his outrageous ravyne.

The gentyl faucoun, that with his feet distrayneth
The kynges hand; the hardy sperhauk eke,
The quayles foo; the merlioun, that payneth

Devyseth describes; *woned* accustomed; *foules of ravyne* birds of prey;
sed seed; *so fele* so many; *perseth* pierces; *clerkes* scholars; *devyse conne*
know how to describe; *tiraunt* tyrant; *donne* dun, dull-brown; *doth*
pyne causes suffering; *ravyne* rapine; *distrayneth* grasps; *sperhauk*
sparrow-hawk; *quayles foo* quail's foe; *merlioun* merlin (small falcon)

Hymself ful ofte the larke for to seke;
There was the douve with hire yën meke;
The jelous swan, ayens his deth that syngeth;
The oule ek, that of deth the bode bryngeth;

The crane, the geaunt, with his trompes soun;
The thef, the chough; and ek the janglynge pye;
The skornynge jay; the eles fo, heroun;
The false lapwynge, ful of trecherye;
The stare, that the conseyl can bewrye;
The tame ruddok, and the coward kyte;
The kok, that orloge is of thorpes lyte;

The sparwe, Venus sone; the nyghtyngale,
That clepeth forth the grene leves newe;
The swalwe, mortherere of the foules smale
That maken hony of floures freshe of hewe;
The wedded turtil, with hire herte trewe;
The pekok, with his aungels fetheres bryghte;
The fesaunt, skornere of the cok by nyghte;

The waker goos; the cukkow ever unkynde;
The popynjay, ful of delicasye;
The drake, stroyere of his owene kynde;

yën meke meek eyes; *ayens* in anticipation of; *ek* also; *bode* omen;
geaunt giant; *thef* thief; *chough* crow; *janglynge pye* chattering magpie;
eles fo eel's foe; *stare* starling; *bewrye* betray; *ruddok* robin redbreast;
orloge timepiece; *thorpes lyte* small villages; *Venus sone* son of Venus;
clepeth calls; *swalwe* swallow; *mortherere of the foules smale* murderer of
bees; *turtil* turtledove; *fesaunt* pheasant: *waker* watchful; *unkynde*
unnatural; *popynjay* parrot; *stroyere* destroyer

The stork, the wrekere of avouterye;
The hote cormeraunt of glotenye;
The raven wys; the crowe with vois of care;
The throstil old; the frosty feldefare.

What shulde I seyn? Of foules every kynde
That in this world han fetheres and stature
Men myghten in that place assembled fynde
Byfore the noble goddesse of Nature,
And everich of hem dide his besy cure
Benygnely to chese or for to take,
By hire acord, his formel or his make.

[Roundel]

Now welcome, somer, with thy sonne softe,
That hast this wintres wedres overshake,
And driven away the longe nyghtes blake!

Saynt Valentyn, that art ful hy on-lofte,
Thus syngen smale foules for thy sake:
Now welcome, somer, with thy sonne softe,
That hast this wintres wedres overshake.

wrekere punisher; *avouterye* adultery; *wys* wise; *throstil* thrush; *frosty*
white-chested; *dide his besy cure* worked diligently; *benygnely*
graciously; *chese* choose; *formel* female (bird); *make* mate; *sonne* sun;
wedres overshake storms shaken off; *on-lofte* on high

THOMAS HEYRICK

On an Indian Tomineios,
the Least of Birds

I'm made in sport by nature, when
  She's tired with the stupendious weight
Of forming elephants and beasts of state:
  Rhinoceros, that love the fen;
  The elks, that scale the hills of snow;
And lions couching in their awful den.
  These do work nature hard, and then
  Her wearied hand in me doth show
What she can for her own diversion do.

Man is a little world ('tis said),
  And I in miniature am drawn,
A perfect creature, but in shorthand shown.
  The ruck, in Madagascar bred
  (If new discoveries truth do speak),
Whom greatest beasts and armèd horsemen dread,
  Both him and me one artist made:
  Nature in this delight doth take,
That can so great and little monsters make.

The Indians me a sunbeam name,
  And I may be the child of one:
So small I am, my kind is hardly known.
  To some a sportive bird I seem,
  And some believe me but a fly;
Though me a feathered fowl the best esteem.
  Whate'er I am, I'm nature's gem,
  And, like a sunbeam from the sky,
I can't be followed by the quickest eye.

I'm the true bird of paradise,
  And heavenly dew's my only meat:
My mouth so small, 'twill nothing else admit.
  No scales know how my weight to poise,
    So light, I seem condensèd air;
And did at the end of the creation rise,
  When nature wanted more supplies,
  When she could little matter spare,
But in return did make the work more rare.

MARY HOWITT

The Dor-Hawk

Fern-owl, Churn-owl, or Goat-sucker,
  Night-jar, Dor-hawk, or whate'er
Be thy name among a dozen, –
Whip-poor-Will's and Who-are-you's cousin,
Chuck-Will's-widow's near relation,
Thou art at thy night vocation,
  Thrilling the still evening air!

In the dark brown wood beyond us,
  Where the night lies dusk and deep;
Where the fox his burrow maketh,
Where the tawny owl awaketh
  Nightly from his day-long sleep;

There Dor-hawk is thy abiding,
  Meadow green is not for thee;
While the aspen branches shiver,
'Mid the roaring of the river,
  Comes thy chirring voice to me.

Bird, thy form I never looked on,
  And to see it do not care;
Thou has been, and thou art only
As a voice of forests lonely,
  Heard and dwelling only there.

Bringing thoughts of dusk and shadow;
  Trees huge-branched in ceaseless change;
Pallid night-moths, spectre-seeming;
All a silent land of dreaming,
  Indistinct and large and strange.

Be thou thus, and thus I prize thee
  More than knowing thee face to face,
Head and beak and leg and feather,
Kept from harm of touch and weather,
  Underneath a fine glass-case.

I can read of thee, and find out
  How thou fliest, fast or slow;
Of thee in the north and south too,
Of thy great moustachioed mouth too,
  And thy Latin name also.

But, Dor-hawk, I love thee better
  While thy voice unto me seems
Coming o'er the evening meadows,
From a dark brown land of shadows,
  Like a pleasant voice of dreams!

ANDREW MOTION

Sparrow

If a sparrow come before my window I take part in its existence and pick about the gravel.
John Keats to Benjamin Bailey, 22 November 1817

No longer
country clubber,
barn bouncer,
hedgerow flasher,
bran dipper,
puddle bather,
dust bowler,
stubble scrounger,
dew nibbler
creeper sleeper,
dung dobbler.
No longer
city slicker,
curb crawler,
gutter weaver,
brick clinger,
dotty mobster,
sill scruffer,
traffic dodger,
drain clogger,
putty pecker,
car bomber.
No longer
daily greeter
scratch singer

piebald shitter,
bib bobber
cocky bugger
boss brawler,
gossip spinner,
crowd pleaser,
heaven filler,
wing dancer.
No longer.

EDWARD THOMAS

The Unknown Bird

Three lovely notes he whistled, too soft to be heard
If others sang; but others never sang
In the great beech-wood all that May and June.
No one saw him: I alone could hear him
Though many listened. Was it but four years
Ago? or five? He never came again.

Oftenest when I heard him I was alone,
Nor could I ever make another hear.
La-la-la! he called seeming far-off –
As if a cock crowed past the edge of the world,
As if the bird or I were in a dream.
Yet that he travelled through the trees and sometimes
Neared me, was plain, though somehow distant still
He sounded. All the proof is – I told men
What I had heard.

           I never knew a voice,
Man, beast, or bird, better than this. I told
The naturalists; but neither had they heard
Anything like the notes that did so haunt me,
I had them clear by heart and have them still.
Four years, or five, have made no difference. Then
As now that La-la-la! was bodiless sweet:
Sad more than joyful it was, if I must say
That it was one or other, but if sad
'Twas sad only with joy too, too far off
For me to taste it. But I cannot tell
If truly never anything but fair

The days were when he sang, as now they seem.
This surely I know, that I who listened then,
Happy sometimes, sometimes suffering
A heavy body and a heavy heart,
Now straightway, if I think of it, become
Light as that bird wandering beyond my shore.

JAMES FENTON

The Orange Dove of Fiji

to R. & B. O'H.

On the slopes of Taveuni
The Barking Pigeons woof
But when I saw the Orange Dove
I nearly hit the roof

And would have surely had there been
A roof around to hit
But the roofs of Taveuni
Are down on the lower bit

While up there in the forest
The Silktails have survived
Where they 'forage in the substage'
And you feel you have *arrived*

As an amateur ornithologist
In the midst of a silktail flock
Until you hear behind you
A 'penetrating tock'

And you find six feet above your head
What you were looking for –
The Orange Dove of Fiji,
No less, no more.

The female of the Orange Dove
Is actually green.

The really orange *male* Orange Dove
Is the one you've seen.

It must have been dipped in Dayglo
Held by its bright green head.
The colour is preposterous.
You want to drop down dead.

It turns around upon its perch
Displaying all the bits
That are mentioned in Dick Watling's book
And the description fits.

Then it says: 'Tock — okay, is that
Enough to convince you yet?
Because that, my friend is all tock tock
That you are going to get.'

Oh the Many-Coloured Fruit Dove
Is pretty enough to boot
And I'm afraid the purple swamphen
Looks queerer than a coot

Like a flagrant English Bishop
Let loose among his flock
With brand-new orange gaiters
(And that's just the swamphen cock)

But the Orange Dove is something
Spectacular to see
So I hope they don't fell another single
Taveuni tree.

SIMON ARMITAGE

The Final Straw

for Peter Bennett

Corn, like the tide coming in. Year on year,
fat, flowing grain, as it had always grown.
We harvested clockwise, spiralling home
over undulations of common land
till nothing remained but a hub of stalks
where the spirit of life was said to lurk.

So childless couples were offered the scythe –
the men invited to pocket the seed,
the women to plait dolls from the last sheaf.

But a Spix's macaw flapped from the blade,
that singular bird of the new world, one
of a kind. A rare sight. And a sign, being
tail-feathers tapering out of view, being

blueness lost in the sun, being gone.

WALT WHITMAN

from Song of Myself

The wild gander leads his flock through the cool night,
Ya-honk he says, and sounds it down to me like an invitation,
The pert may suppose it meaningless, but I listening close,
Find its purpose and place up there toward the wintry sky.

The sharp-hoof'd moose of the north, the cat on the house-
    sill, the chickadee, the prairie-dog,
The litter of the grunting sow as they tug at her teats,
The brood of the turkey-hen and she with her half-spread
    wings,
I see in them and myself the same old law.
The press of my foot to the earth springs a hundred affections,
They scorn the best I can do to relate them.

I am enamour'd of growing out-doors,
Of men that live among cattle or taste of the ocean or woods,
Of the builders and steerers of ships and the wielders of axes
    and mauls, and the drivers of horses,
I can eat and sleep with them week in and week out.

What is commonest, cheapest, nearest, easiest, is Me,
Me going in for my chances, spending for vast returns,
Adorning myself to bestow myself on the first that will take
    me,
Not asking the sky to come down to my good will,
Scattering it freely forever.

MARK DOTY

Flit

         – dart – an idea
arcs the cold, then a clutch

of related thoughts;
slim branches don't even

flicker with the weight
of what's landed;

animate alphabet
whizzing past our faces,

little black and white hurry,
as if a form of notation

accompanied our walk,
a little ahead of us

and a bit behind. If we
could *see* their trajectory,

if their trace remained
in the winter air,

what a tunnel they'd figure:
skein of quick vectors

above our head,
a fierce braid,

improvised, their decisions
— the way one makes poetry

from syntax — unpredictable, resolving
to wild regularity

(thought has to flit
to describe it, speech

has to try that hurry).
A scaffolding,

a kind of argument
about being numerous.

Thread and rethread — alight.
Study. We might be carrying

crumbs. We're not. I wish.
Their small heads cock,

they lift (no visible effort,
as if flight were the work

of the will only), light,
a little further along,

and though they're silent
it seems you could hear

the minute repeating registers
of their attention,

★____, ★____, the *here you are*
yes here you yes.

Pronoun reference unclear.
Who looks at us

– an aerial association
of a dozen subjectivities,

or a singular self
wearing, this snowy afternoon,

twelve pair of wings?
Collectivity of sparks,

sparking collectivity? Say *live*
resides not inside feathers or skin

but in the whizzing medium.
No third person.

Sharp, clear globe of January,
and we – the fourteen of us –

the thinking taking place.
We is instances of alertness,

grammar help me.
Mind in the ringing day,

a little of us ahead
and a bit behind,

and all that action
barely disturbs the air.

JOHN CLARE

To the Snipe

Lover of swamps
And quagmire overgrown
With hassock-tufts of sedge, where fear encamps
Around thy home alone,

The trembling grass
Quakes from the human foot,
Nor bears the weight of man to let him pass
Where thou, alone and mute,

Sittest at rest
In safety, near the clump
Of huge flag-forest that thy haunts invest
Or some old sallow stump,

Thriving on seams
That tiny islands swell,
Just hilling from the mud and rancid streams,
Suiting thy nature well;

For here thy bill,
Suited by wisdom good,
Of rude unseemly length, doth delve and drill
The jellied mass for food;

And here, mayhap,
When summer suns have drest
The moor's rude, desolate and spongy lap,
May hide thy mystic nest —

Mystic indeed;
For isles that oceans make
Are scarcely more secure for birds to build
Than this flag-hidden lake.

Boys thread the woods
To their remotest shades;
But in these marshy flats, these stagnant floods,
Security pervades.

From year to year
Places untrodden lie,
Where man nor boy nor stock hath ventured near,
Naught gazed on but the sky

And fowl that dread
The very breath of man,
Hiding in spots that never knew his tread,
A wild and timid clan,

Widgeon and teal
And wild duck — restless lot,
That from man's dreaded sight will ever steal
To the most dreary spot.

Here tempests howl
Around each flaggy plot,
Where they who dread man's sight, the water fowl,
Hide and are frightened not.

'Tis power divine
That heartens them to brave
The roughest tempest and at ease recline
On marshes or the wave.

Yet instinct knows
Not safety's bounds: – to shun
The firmer ground where skulking fowler goes
With searching dogs and gun,

By tepid springs
Scarcely one stride across
(Though bramble from its edge a shelter flings
Thy safety is at loss)

– And never choose
The little sinky foss,
Streaking the moors whence spa-red water spews
From pudges fringed with moss;

Freebooters there,
Intent to kill or slay,
Startle with cracking guns the trepid air,
And dogs thy haunts betray.

From danger's reach
Here thou art safe to roam,
Far as these washy flag-sown marshes stretch
A still and quiet home.

In these thy haunts
I've gleaned habitual love;
From the vague world where pride and folly taunts
I muse and look above.

Thy solitudes
The unbounded heaven esteems,
And here my heart warms into higher moods
And dignifying dreams.

I see the sky
Smile on the meanest spot,
Giving to all that creep or walk or fly
A calm and cordial lot.

Thine teaches me
Right feelings to employ –
That in the dreariest places peace will be
A dweller and a joy.

JAMIE MCKENDRICK

Right of Way

Were we expecting these toads on our doorstep?
– the smaller with a jewel stuck
to her forehead, a round white pebble,
a third eye, only blind, without a pupil,
picked up on her pilgrimage beside
the artificial lake or risking the ringroad.

It's chill and blank, that stone – perhaps a chunk
of granite ballast from the virtual quarry,
the way it seems more of an ailment
than an ornament. Her mate is clad in
eco-warrior fatigues: grey chevrons
screenprinted on a ground of dull jade.

Both have a furtive, raddled air as if
in protest at the dust fumes and the din
as the grabclaw clanks on the wagons' rim,
loading and unloading ballast. But the door open,
they make for the hallway with sagging hops
like small encrusted beanbags on the move

and seem to know, thanks all the same,
where the back door is, like it was their
house, or no house at all – their right of way
from well before we'd made such strides ahead
as building walls to live inside of, theirs before
we'd dragged our pelts and selves out of the mud.

ROBINSON JEFFERS

Carmel Point

The extraordinary patience of things!
This beautiful place defaced with a crop of suburban houses –
How beautiful when we first beheld it,
Unbroken field of poppy and lupin walled with clean cliffs;
No intrusion but two or three horses pasturing,
Or a few milch cows rubbing their flanks on the outcrop
  rockheads –
Now the spoiler has come: does it care?
Not faintly. It has all time. It knows the people are a tide
That swells and in time will ebb, and all
Their works dissolve. Meanwhile the image of the pristine
  beauty
Lives in the very grain of the granite,
Safe as the endless ocean that climbs our cliff. – As for us:
We must uncenter our minds from ourselves;
We must unhumanize our views a little, and become
  confident
As the rock and ocean that we were made from.

GERARD MANLEY HOPKINS

Inversnaid

This darksome burn, horseback brown,
His rollrock highroad roaring down,
In coop and in comb the fleece of his foam
Flutes and low to the lake falls home.

A windpuff-bonnet of fáwn-fróth
Turns and twindles over the broth
Of a pool so pitchblack, féll-frówning,
It rounds and rounds Despair to drowning.

Degged with dew, dappled with dew
Are the groins of the braes that the brook treads through,
Wiry heathpacks, flitches of fern,
And the beadbonny ash that sits over the burn.

What would the world be, once bereft
Of wet and of wilderness? Let them be left,
O let them be left, wildness and wet;
Long live the weeds and the wilderness yet.

SEAMUS HEANEY

On the Spot

A cold clutch, a whole nestful, all but hidden
In last year's autumn leaf mould, and I knew
By the mattness and the stillness of them, rotten,
Making death-sweat of a morning dew
That didn't so much shine the shells as damp them.
I was down on my hands and knees in the wet
Grass under the hedge, adoring it,
Early riser busy reaching in
And used to finding warm eggs. But instead
This sudden polar stud
And stigma and dawn stone-circle chill
In my mortified right hand, proof positive
Of what conspired on the spot to addle
Matter in its planetary stand-off.

C. K. WILLIAMS

Tar

The first morning of Three Mile Island: those first disquieting,
     uncertain, mystifying hours.
All morning a crew of workmen have been tearing the old
     decrepit roof off our building,
and all morning, trying to distract myself, I've been wandering
     out to watch them
as they hack away the leaden layers of asbestos paper and
     disassemble the disintegrating drains.
After half a night of listening to the news, wondering how to
     know a hundred miles downwind
if and when to make a run for it and where, then a coming bolt
     awake at seven
when the roofers we've been waiting for since winter sent their
     ladders shrieking up our wall,
we still know less than nothing: the utility company continues
     making little of the accident,
the slick federal spokesmen still have their evasions in some
     semblance of order.
Surely we suspect now we're being lied to, but in the
     meantime, there are the roofers,
setting winch-frames, sledging rounds of tar apart, and there I
     am, on the curb across, gawking.

I never realised what brutal work it is, how matter-of-factly and
     harrowingly dangerous.
The ladders flex and quiver, things skid from the edge, the
     materials are bulky and recalcitrant.
When the rusty, antique nails are levered out, their heads pull
     off; the underroofing crumbles.

Even the battered little furnace, roaring along as patient as a
donkey, chokes and clogs,
a dense, malignant smoke shoots up, and someone has to fiddle
with a cock, then hammer it,
before the gush and stench will deintensify, the dark, Dantean
broth wearily subside.
In its crucible, the stuff looks bland, like licorice, spill it,
though, on your boots or coveralls,
it sears, and everything is permeated with it, the furnace
gunked with burst and half-burst bubbles,
the men themselves so completely slashed and mucked they
seem almost from another realm, like trolls.
When they take their break, they leave their brooms standing
at attention in the asphalt pails,
work gloves clinging like Br'er Rabbit to the bitten shafts, and
they slouch along the precipitous lip,
the enormous sky behind them, the heavy noontime air alive
with shimmers and mirages.

Sometime in the afternoon I had to go inside: the advent of our
vigil was upon us.
However much we didn't want to, however little we would do
about it, we'd understood:
we were going to perish of all this, if not now, then soon, if not
soon, then someday.
Someday, some final generation, hysterically aswarm beneath
an atmosphere as unrelenting as rock,
would rue us all, anathematize our earthly comforts, curse our
surfeits and submissions.
I think I know, though I might rather not, why my roofers stay
so clear to me and why the rest,
the terror of that time, the reflexive disbelief and distancing, all
we should hold on to, dims so.
I remember the president in his absurd protective booties,
looking absolutely unafraid, the fool.

I remember a woman on the front page glaring across the
  misty Susquehanna at those looming stacks.

But, more vividly, the men, silvered with glitter from the
  shingles, clinging like starlings beneath the eaves.

Even the leftover carats of tar in the gutter, so black they
  seemed to suck the light out of the air.

By nightfall kids had come across them: every sidewalk on the
  block was scribbled with obscenities and hearts.

EDWIN MUIR

The Horses

Barely a twelvemonth after
The seven days war that put the world to sleep,
Late in the evening the strange horses came.
By then we had made our covenant with silence,
But in the first few days it was so still
We listened to our breathing and were afraid.
On the second day
The radios failed; we turned the knobs; no answer.
On the third day a warship passed us, heading north,
Dead bodies piled on the deck. On the sixth day
A plane plunged over us into the sea. Thereafter
Nothing. The radios dumb;
And still they stand in corners of our kitchens,
And stand, perhaps, turned on, in a million rooms
All over the world. But now if they should speak,
If on a sudden they should speak again,
If on the stroke of noon a voice should speak,
We would not listen, we would not let it bring
That old bad world that swallowed its children quick
At one great gulp. We would not have it again.
Sometimes we think of the nations lying asleep,
Curled blindly in impenetrable sorrow,
And then the thought confounds us with its strangeness.
The tractors lie about our fields; at evening
They look like dank sea-monsters couched and waiting.
We leave them where they are and let them rust:
'They'll moulder away and be like other loam.'

We make our oxen drag our rusty ploughs,
Long laid aside. We have gone back
Far past our fathers' land.
                              And then, that evening
Late in the summer the strange horses came.
We heard a distant tapping on the road,
A deepening drumming; it stopped, went on again
And at the corner changed to hollow thunder.
We saw the heads
Like a wild wave charging and were afraid.
We had sold our horses in our fathers' time
To buy new tractors. Now they were strange to us
As fabulous steeds set on an ancient shield
Or illustrations in a book of knights.
We did not dare go near them. Yet they waited,
Stubborn and shy, as if they had been sent
By an old command to find our whereabouts
And that long-lost archaic companionship.
In the first moment we had never a thought
That they were creatures to be owned and used.
Among them were some half-a-dozen colts
Dropped in some wilderness of the broken world,
Yet new as if they had come from their own Eden.
Since then they have pulled our ploughs and borne our loads,
But that free servitude still can pierce our hearts.
Our life is changed; their coming our beginning.

LAVINIA GREENLAW

The Recital of Lost Cities

It started with the polar ice caps.
A slight increase in temperature and the quiet
was shattered. The Australian Antarctic
wandered all over the Norwegian Dependency
as mountainous fragments lurched free
with a groan like ship's mahogany.

And then there was the continental shift:
everywhere you went, America was coming closer.
Hot weather brought plague and revolution.
Nations disappeared or renamed themselves
as borders moved, in, out, in, out,
with tidal persistence and threat.

Cartographers dealt in picture postcards.
The printing plates for the last atlas
were archived unused. Their irrelevant contours
gathered dust, locked in a vault
to save the public from the past
and the danger of wrong directions.

The sea rose by inches, unravelled the coastline,
eased across the lowlands and licked at the hills
where people gathered to remember names:
Calcutta, Tokyo, San Francisco,
Venice, Amsterdam, Baku,
Alexandria, Santo Domingo ...

THOMAS HOOD

The Sea of Death
A fragment

              Methought I saw
Life swiftly treading over endless space;
And, at her foot-print, but a bygone pace,
The ocean-past, which, with increasing wave,
Swallow'd her steps like a pursuing grave.
Sad were my thoughts that anchor'd silently
On the dead waters of that passionless sea,
Unstirr'd by any touch of living breath:
Silence hung over it, and drowsy Death,
Like a gorged sea-bird, slept with folded wings
On crowded carcases – sad passive things
That wore the thin grey surface, like a veil
Over the calmness of their features pale.

And there were Spring-faced cherubs that did sleep
Like water-lilies on that motionless deep,
How beautiful! with bright unruffled hair
On sleek unfretted brows, and eyes that were
Buried in marble tombs, a pale eclipse!
And smile-bedimpled cheeks, and pleasant lips,
Meekly apart, as if the soul intense
Spake out in dreams of its own innocence:
And so they lay in loveliness and kept
The birth-night of their peace, that Life e'en wept
With very envy of their happy fronts;
For there were neighbour brows scarr'd by the brunts
Of strife and sorrowing – where Care had set
His crooked autograph, and marr'd the jet

Of glossy locks with hollow eyes forlorn,
And lips that curl'd in bitterness and scorn –
Wretched, – as they had breath'd of this world's pain,
And so bequeath'd it to the world again
Through the beholder's heart with heavy sighs.

So lay they garmented in torpid light,
Under the pall of a transparent night,
Like solemn apparitions lull'd sublime
To everlasting rest, – and with them Time
Slept, as he sleeps upon the silent face
Of a dark dial in a sunless place.

GEORGE GORDON, LORD BYRON

Darkness

I had a dream, which was not all a dream.
The bright sun was extinguish'd, and the stars
Did wander darkling in the eternal space,
Rayless, and pathless, and the icy earth
Swung blind and blackening in the moonless air;
Morn came and went – and came, and brought no day,
And men forgot their passions in the dread
Of this their desolation; and all hearts
Were chill'd into a selfish prayer for light:
And they did live by watchfires – and the thrones,
The palaces of crowned kings – the huts,
The habitations of all things which dwell,
Were burnt for beacons; cities were consumed,
And men were gather'd round their blazing homes
To look once more into each other's face;
Happy were those who dwelt within the eye
Of the volcanos, and their mountain-torch:
A fearful hope was all the world contain'd;
Forests were set on fire – but hour by hour
They fell and faded – and the crackling trunks
Extinguish'd with a crash – and all was black.
The brows of men by the despairing light
Wore an unearthly aspect, as by fits
The flashes fell upon them; some lay down
And hid their eyes and wept; and some did rest
Their chins upon their clenched hands, and smiled;
And others hurried to and fro, and fed
Their funeral piles with fuel, and look'd up
With mad disquietude on the dull sky,

The pall of a past world; and then again
With curses cast them down upon the dust,
And gnash'd their teeth and howl'd: the wild birds shriek'd,
And, terrified, did flutter on the ground,
And flap their useless wings; the wildest brutes
Came tame and tremulous; and vipers crawl'd
And twined themselves among the multitude,
Hissing, but stingless – they were slain for food:
And War, which for a moment was no more,
Did glut himself again; – a meal was bought
With blood, and each sate sullenly apart
Gorging himself in gloom: no love was left;
All earth was but one thought – and that was death,
Immediate and inglorious; and the pang
Of famine fed upon all entrails – men
Died, and their bones were tombless as their flesh;
The meagre by the meagre were devour'd,
Even dogs assail'd their masters, all save one,
And he was faithful to a corse, and kept
The birds and beasts and famish'd men at bay,
Till hunger clung them, or the dropping dead
Lured their lank jaws; himself sought out no food,
But with a piteous and perpetual moan,
And a quick desolate cry, licking the hand
Which answer'd not with a caress – he died.
The crowd was famish'd by degrees; but two
Of an enormous city did survive,
And they were enemies: they met beside
The dying embers of an altar-place
Where had been heap'd a mass of holy things
For an unholy usage; they raked up,
And shivering scraped with their cold skeleton hands
The feeble ashes, and their feeble breath
Blew for a little life, and made a flame
Which was a mockery; then they lifted up

Their eyes as it grew lighter, and beheld
Each other's aspects – saw, and shriek'd, and died –
Even of their mutual hideousness they died,
Unknowing who he was upon whose brow
Famine had written Fiend. The world was void,
The populous and the powerful was a lump,
Seasonless, herbless, treeless, manless, lifeless –
A lump of death – a chaos of hard clay.
The rivers, lakes, and ocean all stood still,
And nothing stirr'd within their silent depths;
Ships sailorless lay rotting on the sea,
And their masts fell down piecemeal; as they dropp'd
They slept on the abyss without a surge –
The waves were dead; the tides were in their grave,
The Moon, their mistress, had expired before;
The winds were wither'd in the stagnant air,
And the clouds perish'd; Darkness had no need
Of aid from them – She was the Universe.

CHRISTOPHER REID

A Pub Band

Behold the World, how it is whirled round,
And for it is so whirl'd, is named so.
Sir John Davies, 'Orchestra'

From where we stand
this spinning ball
our mother earth
it's all dark backward
and abysm
so to speak
so far as birth

The moon her bleak
sister or daughter
we're told sprang
out of some casual
cataclysm
a bump in the night
a bit of a fright

So far so bad
and in the light
the light of the dark
backward etcetera
isn't it enough
that nub of the night sky
to be getting on with

No not enough
we need to know
not just the dry
fact of the moon
but a better myth
more outlandish truth
to help explain us

Numbers numb us
tell us nothing
we can feel
the clock's not real
always a tick
away from midnight
an empty trick

Better rather
enjoy the spacious
dance of the planets
igneous gaseous
far out or farther
these carbuncles
our aunts and uncles

And their father
or mother sun
from whom they were spun
and other suns
that splash the dark
inviting assent
from our infinitesimal spark

W. H. AUDEN

Ode to Gaea

From this new culture of the air we finally see,
far-shining in excellence, what our Mother, the
      nicest daughter of Chaos, would
   admire could she look in a glass,

and what, in her eyes, is natural: it is the old
grand style of gesture we watch as, heavy with cold,
      the top-waters of all her
   northern seas take their vernal plunge,

and suddenly her desolations, salt as blood,
prolix yet terse, are glamorously carpeted
      with great swatches of plankton,
   delicious spreads of nourishment,

while, in her realm of solids, lively dots expand,
companionship becomes an unstaid passion and
      leaves by the mile hide tons of
   pied pebbles that will soon be birds.

Now that we know how she looks, she seems more mysterious
than when, in her *partibus infidelibus*,
      we painted sizzling dragons
   and wizards reading upside down,

but less approachable: where she joins girl's-ear lakes
to bird's-foot deltas with lead-blue squiggles she makes,
      surely, a value judgment,
   'of pure things Water is the best,'

but how does she rank wheelwrights? One doubts if she knows
which sub-species of folly is peculiar to those
     pretty molehills, where on that
    pocket-handkerchief of a plain

the syntax changes: peering down sleepily at
a crenellated shore, the tired old diplomat
     becomes embarrassed – Should he
    smile for 'our great good ally', scowl

at 'that vast and detestable empire' or choose
the sneer reserved for certain Southern countries 'whose
     status and moral climate
    we have no desire, sir, to emulate'?

But why we should feel neglected on mountain drives,
unpopular in woods, is quite clear; the older lives
     have no wish to be stood in
    rows or at right angles: below,

straight as its railroads, cutting diagonally across
a positivist republic, two lines of moss
     show where the Devil's Causeway
    drew pilgrims thirteen gods ago,

and on this eve of whispers and tapped telephones
before the Ninth Catastrophe, square corner-stones
     still distinguish a fortress
    of the High Kings from untutored rock.

Tempting to mortals is the fancy of half-concerned
Gods in the sky, of a bored Thunderer who turned
     from the Troy-centred grief to
    watch the Hippemolgoi drink their milk,

and how plausible from his look-point: we may well
shake a weak fist one day at this vision, but the spell
    of high places will haunt us
     long after our jaunt has declined,

as soon it must, to the hard ground. Where six foot is tall,
good-manners will ask easy riddles like 'Why are all
    the rowdiest marches and the
     most venomous iambics composed

by lame clergymen?', will tell no tales which end in worse
disaster than that of the tipsy poet who cursed
    a baby for whom later
     he came to sigh. So we were taught

before the Greater Engines came and the police
who go with them, when the long rivers ran through peace
    and the holy laws of Speech were
     held in awe, even by evil tongues,

and manners, maybe, will stand us in better stead,
down there, than a kantian conscience. From overhead
    much harm is discernible,
     farms unroofed and harbour-works wrecked

in the Second Assault; frank to an ungrieving sky
as still they look, too many fertilities lie
    in dread of the tormentor's
     fondling finger, and in the few

that still have poky shops and audiences of one,
many are overweight, the pious peasant's only son,
    goading their crumpled faces
     down innocence-corrupting roads,

dreams of cities where his cows are whores. When the wise
wilt in the glare of the Shadow, the stern advise
      tribute, and the large-hearted
   already talk Its gibberish,

perhaps a last stand in the passes will be made
by those whose Valhalla would be hearing verse by Praed
      or arias by Rossini
   between two entrées by Carême.

We hope so. But who on Cupid's Coming would care to bet?
More than one World's Bane has been scotched before this, yet
      Justice during his *Te Deum*
   slipped away sighing from the hero's pew,

and Earth, till the end, will be Herself. She has never been moved
except by Amphion, and orators have not improved
      since misled Athens perished
   upon Sicilian marble: what,

to Her, the real one, can our good landscapes be but lies,
those woods where tigers chum with deer and no root dies,
      that tideless bay where children
   play Bishop on a golden shore?

BILLY COLLINS

As If to Demonstrate an Eclipse

I pick an orange from a wicker basket
and place it on the table
to represent the sun.
Then down at the other end
a blue and white marble
becomes the earth
and nearby I lay the little moon of an aspirin.

I get a glass from a cabinet,
open a bottle of wine,
then I sit in a ladder-back chair,
a benevolent god presiding
over a miniature creation myth,

and I begin to sing
a homemade canticle of thanks
for this perfect little arrangement,
for not making the earth too hot or cold
not making it spin too fast or slow

so that the grove of orange trees
and the owl become possible,
not to mention the rolling wave,
the play of clouds, geese in flight,
and the Z of lightning on a dark lake.

Then I fill my glass again
and give thanks for the trout,
the oak, and the yellow feather,

singing the room full of shadows,
as sun and earth and moon
circle one another in their impeccable orbits
and I get more and more cockeyed with gratitude.

WILLIAM BLAKE

Auguries of Innocence

To see a World in a Grain of Sand
And a Heaven in a Wild Flower,
Hold Infinity in the palm of your hand
And Eternity in an hour.

A Robin Red breast in a Cage
Puts all Heaven in a Rage.
A dove house fill'd with doves & Pigeons
Shudders Hell thro' all its regions.
A dog starv'd at his Masters' Gate
Predicts the ruin of the State.
A Horse misus'd upon the Road
Calls to Heaven for Human blood.
Each outcry of the hunted Hare
A fibre from the Brain does tear.
A Skylark wounded in the wing,
A Cherubim does cease to sing.
The Game Cock clip'd & arm'd for fight
Does the Rising Sun affright.
Every Wolf's & Lion's howl
Raises from Hell a Human Soul.
The wild deer, wand'ring here & there,
Keeps the Human Soul from Care.
The Lamb misus'd breeds Public strife
And yet forgives the Butcher's Knife.
The Bat that flits at close of Eve
Has left the Brain that won't Believe.
The Owl that calls upon the Night
Speaks the Unbeliever's fright.

He who shall hurt the little Wren
Shall never be belov'd by Men.
He who the Ox to wrath has mov'd
Shall never be by Woman lov'd.
The wanton Boy that kills the Fly
Shall feel the Spider's enmity.
He who torments the Chafer's sprite
Weaves a Bower in endless Night.
The Catterpiller on the Leaf
Repeats to thee thy Mother's grief.
Kill not the Moth nor Butterfly,
For the Last Judgment draweth nigh.
He who shall train the Horse to War
Shall never pass the Polar Bar.
The Begger's Dog & Widow's Cat,
Feed them & thou wilt grow fat.
The Gnat that sings his Summer's song
Poison gets from Slander's tongue.
The poison of the Snake & Newt
Is the sweat of Envy's Foot.
The Poison of the Honey Bee
Is the Artist's Jealousy.
The Prince's Robes & Beggar's Rags
Are Toadstools on the Miser's Bags.
A truth that's told with bad intent
Beats all the Lies you can invent.
It is right it should be so;
Man was made for Joy & Woe;
And when this we rightly know
Thro' the World we safely go.
Joy & Woe are woven fine,
A Clothing for the Soul divine;
Under every grief & pine
Runs a joy with silken twine.
The Babe is more than swadling Bands;

Throughout all these Human Lands
Tools were made, & Born were hands,
Every Farmer Understands.
Every Tear from Every Eye
Becomes a Babe in Eternity;
This is caught by Females bright
And return'd to its own delight.
The Bleat, the Bark, Bellow & Roar
Are Waves that Beat on Heaven's Shore.
The Babe that weeps the Rod beneath
Writes Revenge in realms of death.
The Beggar's Rags, fluttering in Air,
Does to Rags the Heavens tear.
The Soldier, arm'd with Sword & Gun,
Palsied strikes the Summer's Sun.
The poor Man's Farthing is worth more
Than all the Gold on Afric's Shore.
One Mite wrung from the Labrer's hands
Shall buy & sell the Miser's Lands:
Or, if protected from on high,
Does that whole Nation sell & buy.
He who mocks the Infant's Faith
Shall be mock'd in Age & Death.
He who shall teach the Child to Doubt
The rotting Grave shall ne'er get out.
He who respects the Infant's faith
Triumphs over Hell & Death.
The Child's Toys & the Old Man's Reasons
Are the Fruits of the Two seasons.
The Questioner, who sits so sly,
Shall never know how to Reply.
He who replies to words of Doubt
Doth put the Light of Knowledge out.
The Strongest Poison ever known
Came from Caesar's Laurel Crown.

Nought can deform the Human Race
Like to the Armour's iron brace.
When Gold & Gems adorn the Plow
To peaceful Arts shall Envy Bow.
A Riddle or the Cricket's Cry
Is to Doubt a fit Reply.
The Emmet's Inch & Eagle's Mile
Make Lame Philosophy to smile.
He who Doubts from what he sees
Will ne'er Believe, do what you Please.
If the Sun & Moon should doubt,
They'd immediately Go out.
To be in a Passion you Good may do,
But no Good if a Passion is in you.
The Whore & Gambler, by the State
Licenc'd, build that Nation's Fate.
The Harlot's cry from Street to Street
Shall weave Old England's winding Sheet.
The Winner's Shout, the Loser's Curse,
Dance before dead England's Hearse.
Every Night & every Morn
Some to Misery are Born.
Every Morn & every Night
Some are Born to sweet delight.
Some are Born to sweet delight,
Some are Born to Endless Night.
We are led to Believe a Lie
When we see [With *del.*] not Thro' the Eye
Which was Born in a Night to perish in a Night
When the Soul Slept in Beams of Light.
God Appears & God is Light
To those poor Souls who dwell in Night,
But does a Human Form Display
To those who Dwell in Realms of day.

W. B. YEATS

To a Squirrel at Kyle-na-no

Come play with me;
Why should you run
Through the shaking tree
As though I'd a gun
To strike you dead?
When all I would do
Is to scratch your head
And let you go.

ELIZABETH BISHOP

The Armadillo

for Robert Lowell

This is the time of year
when almost every night
the frail, illegal fire balloons appear.
Climbing the mountain height,

rising toward a saint
still honored in these parts,
the paper chambers flush and fill with light
that comes and goes, like hearts.

Once up against the sky it's hard
to tell them from the stars —
planets, that is — the tinted ones:
Venus going down, or Mars,

or the pale green one. With a wind,
they flare and falter, wobble and toss;
but if it's still they steer between
the kite sticks of the Southern Cross,

receding, dwindling, solemnly
and steadily forsaking us,
or, in the downdraft from a peak,
suddenly turning dangerous.

Last night another big one fell.
It splattered like an egg of fire
against the cliff behind the house.
The flame ran down. We saw the pair

of owls who nest there flying up
and up, their whirling black-and-white
stained bright pink underneath, until
they shrieked up out of sight.

The ancient owls' nest must have burned.
Hastily, all alone,
a glistening armadillo left the scene,
rose-flecked, head down, tail down,

and then a baby rabbit jumped out,
short-eared, to our surprise.
So soft! – a handful of intangible ash
with fixed, ignited eyes.

Too pretty, dreamlike mimicry!
O falling fire and piercing cry
and panic, and a weak mailed fist
clenched ignorant against the sky!

ROBERT CRAWFORD

The Bad Shepherd

I am the bad shepherd, torching my flocks in the fields,
Feeding them accelerant, hecatombs of wedders and tups.
In pits or pyres all are sheared and shamed by the flames.
Every sheep is a black sheep in that fire,
Penned in by heat, conspicuously consumed.
If one escapes when ninety-nine are burned,
Hunt it down. Best now my lambs are lost
So sheep are shelved, or vaporised unsold,
Hanging in charred clouds – hairst hogs, maillies, and crocks.
Cloned palls cover Cumbria. Shadows slur Lockerbie's drumlins.
Cling, braxy, scrapie, tremmlin, pindling, all
Diseases of sheep go huddled together in one
Beltane burn. *Ca' the yowes to the knowes* ...
I am the bad shepherd. Follow me.

ROBERT WRIGLEY

The Gift of the Bear

for R.C.

Would you believe a man if he claimed
it was not spring? He'd admit there were birds,
not beyond counting, but beyond the words
any distracted soul might use to name

how many there were. Nuthatches, he'd know,
and chickadees, in a pure winter sun
so warm and snowless the window was open,
which was why he heard them singing so.

Would you believe him if he said
that in the midst of this January
flurry of songbirds, a bear, unwary,
dull, and awkwardly stumbling, had emerged

from the woods just east of the house and caught
the scent as it came of the bird feeder
there — a thatch of seeds inside its cedar
walls, and at either end, in wire, the store-bought

slabs of suet just recently replaced,
each with only a faint beak divot or two.
Would you believe him if he said to you
he had watched all this from his own warm place

in the bedroom, with his wife, making love?
Forgive him. For saying too honest a thing,
or too private a thing, at least, might seem
wrong in a way, or in the blessings of

such weather, or blessed by such a woman
as the one who lay eyes closed before him,
since she was the one for whom weather's conundrum
was still only birdsong, odd warmth, a man.

But do you believe him? He never said
a word to her about the bear, who leaned
against the expensive steel feeder stand
and bent the thing down as if it were lead,

who grunted then and hooked a black deft claw
first in the one wire bail that held the suet
and then the other, unloosing four notes
each time as staples twanged around its paw.

Would you believe it? Could you imagine
the ecstasy that bear came to know
there? Those cakes of roasted seed and tallow,
the way it sat back and held them, each one,

to its snout, with both paws, contentedly
mouthing. Do you understand when the man says
it was neither spring nor silent that day?
though soon enough it was January

again, and the snow drifted deep that side
of the house, and the arc of the bent stand
and the broken feeder both disappeared
until spring came for real this time and stayed.

Which is the source of the secret you've been told
today. How it seems to the woman
he loves an oddity, not an omen,
that weird, barely shaped, two peninsulated

wild knot of greens the spilled seeds have grown to.
He has straightened the stand, fixed the feeder's bails,
and he's kept from her nothing else at all —
only the bear, which now, he gives to you.

EMILY DICKINSON

'Further in Summer than the Birds'

Further in Summer than the Birds
Pathetic from the Grass
A minor Nation celebrates
Its unobtrusive Mass.

No Ordinance be seen
So gradual the Grace
A pensive Custom it becomes
Enlarging Loneliness.

Antiquest felt at Noon
When August burning low
Arise this spectral Canticle
Repose to typify

Remit as yet no Grace
No Furrow on the Glow
Yet a Druidic Difference
Enhances Nature now

SEAMUS HEANEY

St Kevin and the Blackbird

And then there was St Kevin and the blackbird.
The saint is kneeling, arms stretched out, inside
His cell, but the cell is narrow, so

One turned-up palm is out the window, stiff
As a crossbeam, when a blackbird lands
And lays in it and settles down to nest.

Kevin feels the warm eggs, the small breast, the tucked
Neat head and claws and, finding himself linked
Into the network of eternal life,

Is moved to pity: now he must hold his hand
Like a branch out in the sun and rain for weeks
Until the young are hatched and fledged and flown.

★

And since the whole thing's imagined anyhow,
Imagine being Kevin. Which is he?
Self-forgetful or in agony all the time

From the neck on out down through his hurting forearms?
Are his fingers sleeping? Does he still feel his knees?
Or has the shut-eyed blank of underearth

Crept up through him? Is there distance in his head?
Alone and mirrored clear in love's deep river,
'To labour and not to seek reward,' he prays,

A prayer his body makes entirely
For he has forgotten self, forgotten bird
And on the riverbank forgotten the river's name.

GALWAY KINNELL

Saint Francis and the Sow

The bud
stands for all things,
even for those things that don't flower,
for everything flowers, from within, of self-blessing;
though sometimes it is necessary
to reteach a thing its loveliness,
to put a hand on its brow
of the flower
and retell it in words and in touch
it is lovely
until it flowers again from within, of self-blessing;
as Saint Francis
put his hand on the creased forehead
of the sow, and told her in words and in touch
blessings of earth on the sow, and the sow
began remembering all down her thick length,
from the earthen snout all the way
through the fodder and slops to the spiritual curl of the tail,
from the hard spininess spiked out from the spine
down through the great broken heart
to the sheer blue milken dreaminess spurting and shuddering
from the fourteen teats into the fourteen mouths sucking and
    blowing beneath them:
the long, perfect loveliness of sow.

JORIE GRAHAM

Love

Here it's harvest. Dust
  coarsens
the light. In the heat
  in the distance
the men burn
  their fields

to heal them. The grass
  is tall.
They disappear,
  they reappear ...
slowly they navigate
  by fire,

cutting a path
  of ash.
They beat
  the flames
then lean
  on their tall forks

and stare. Nearby
  the sheep
in a stunned unison
  work what
remains. Dogs bite
  the strays.

What stark thing
  is it

we want
    that's only visible, believable,
caught through
    this blinding

yield? What poverty
    is strict enough?
Eight hundred years
    ago
in these fields
    the man

known as Saint
    Francis
abandoned by his
    church
and going blind
    spent all

one night. The medicine,
    the light
of his time,
    saw fit to burn him
at the temples
    to restore sight,

and all the tiny veins
    from ear to eye,
out of tremendous love,
    were cut.
It didn't work,
    but in great pain

near here, one night,
    the story goes,
rats worried him,
    visiting

his helpless warmth.
  To see them

for what they were,
  old man,
he composed
  in the dark
his famous
  canticle – *brother*

sunlight, brother
  firelight. The rats
traveled his face
  eating
the open scars. Later
  his blessèd

aides bore through both ears
  with red hot irons
to no avail
  for sight. *Harm not*
the fire
  he said

to those who would
  save him,
and never would he, did he,
  extinguish
a candle,
  a lantern,

with so much
  pity
was he moved
  toward it.

DERYN REES-JONES

Trilobite

Remember, as a child, how someone would shout *Catch!*
and too old to refuse, and too young not to,
the body's coordinates not quite set,

this object, moving in an arc towards you
somehow created you, trembling, outstretched?
That's how it came to me, this trilobite,

a present from the underworld, a stern familiar
hopelessly far-fetched. What it wanted from me
I never knew, its hard parts being its only parts,

the three sections of its crossways nature
– *cephalon, thorax, pygidium*
as later, now, I've learned to call them,

carrying a memory of themselves like water
as my fingers moved on its captive body,
the feathery stone of its cool guitar.

It reminded me of a woodlouse, too,
the honesty of small, friendly things.
But the metallic gleam of its smoothed edges

were taut and innocent as an unfired gun.
So it bedded in, leaving behind a gleaming trail
as a biro bleeding in a pocket might,

a puff of ink from a hounded squid.
And my skin shimmered
with its silvery threads, and my breath quickened

as it wrote my body, left a garden of knowing in damp tattoos.
The further I threw it, the closer it came.
Sometimes, alone, I'd ask it questions

stroke it like a secret pet
How deep is the ocean? What's the blueness of blue?
How is the earth as you lie inside it?

It would reply in a voice both
high-pitched and enduring, or
whisper like a ghost till only breath remained.

And left me only when I'd learned to love it,
small as a bullethole,
in the place where it pressed itself,

its fossil colours close to my heart.
Last night, unable to sleep,
it nudged its way back into my life,

pulling me from the fragrant pillow
to perch once again on my naked shoulders,
to drop like a coin in my offered hand.

Beside me, my husband slept.
And the fact of its presence, its subtle truth,
was something to touch,

like the wounds of Christ.
Its transformation as I went to kiss it,
a wafer on the pushed out tongue.

EMILY DICKINSON

'The Gentian weaves her fringes'

The Gentian weaves her fringes –
The Maple's loom is red –
My departing blossoms
    Obviate parade.

A brief, but patient illness –
An hour to prepare,
And one below this morning
Is where the angels are –
It was a short procession,
The Bobolink was there –
An aged Bee addressed us –
And then we knelt in prayer –
We trust that she was willing –
We ask that we may be.
Summer – Sister – Seraph!
Let us go with thee!

In the name of the Bee –
And of the Butterfly –
And of the Breeze – Amen!

ALEXANDER WILSON

The Fisherman's Hymn

The osprey sails above the sound,
The geese are gone, the gulls are flying;
The herring shoals swarm thick around,
The nets are launched, the boats are plying.
Yo ho, my hearts! let's seek the deep,
Raise high the song and cheerly wish her,
Still as the bending net we sweep,
'God bless the fish-hawk and the fisher!'
She brings us fish – she brings us Spring,
Good times, fair weather, warmth, and plenty;
Fine store of shad, trout, herring, ling,
Sheep-head and drum, and old wives' dainty.
Yo ho, my hearts! let's seek the deep,
Ply every oar, and cheerly wish her,
Still as the bending net we sweep,
'God bless the fish-hawk and the fisher!'
She rears her young on yonder tree,
She leaves her faithful mate to mind 'em;
Like us, for fish she sails the sea,
And, plunging, shows us where to find 'em.
Yo ho, my hearts! let's seek the deep,
Ply every oar, and cheerly wish her,
while slow the bending net we sweep,
'God bless the fish-hawk and the fisher!'

SAMUEL TAYLOR COLERIDGE

from The Rime of the Ancient Mariner

Part IV

'I fear thee, ancient Mariner!
I fear thy skinny hand!
And thou are long, and lank, and brown,
As is the ribbed sea-sand.

The Wedding-Guest
feareth that a Spirit is
talking to him;

I fear thee and thy glittering eye,
And thy skinny hand, so brown.' –
Fear not, fear not, thou Wedding-Guest!
This body dropt not down.

But the ancient
Mariner assureth him
of his bodily life, and
proceedeth to relate
his horrible penance.

Alone, alone, all, all alone,
Alone on a wide wide sea!
And never a saint took pity on
My soul in agony.

The many men, so beautiful!
And they all dead did lie:
And a thousand thousand slimy things
Lived on; and so did I.

He despiseth the
creatures of the calm,

I looked upon the rotting sea,
And drew my eyes away;
I looked upon the rotting deck,
And there the dead men lay.

And envieth that *they*
should live and so
many lie dead.

I looked to heaven, and tried to pray;
But or ever a prayer had gusht,
A wicked whisper came, and made
My heart as dry as dust.

I closed my lids, and kept them close,
And the balls like pulses beat;
For the sky and the sea, and the sea and the sky
Lay like a load on my weary eye,
And the dead were at my feet.

The cold sweat melted from their limbs,
Nor rot nor reek did they:
The look with which they looked on me
Had never passed away.

But the curse liveth for him in the eye of the dead men.

An orphan's curse would drag to hell
A spirit from on high;
But oh! more horrible than that
Is the curse in a dead man's eye!
Seven days, seven nights, I saw that curse,
And yet I could not die.

The moving Moon went up the sky,
And no where did abide:
Softly she was going up,
And a star or two beside –

In his loneliness and fixedness he yearneth towards the journeying Moon, and the stars that still sojourn, yet still move onward; and every where the blue sky belongs to them, and is their appointed rest, and their native country and their own natural homes, which they enter unannounced, as lords that are certainly expected and yet there is a silent joy at their arrival.

Her beams bemocked the sultry main,
Like April hoar-frost spread;
But where the ship's huge shadow lay,
The charmèd water burnt alway
A still and awful red.

Beyond the shadow of the ship,
I watched the water-snakes:
They moved in tracks of shining white,
And when they reared, the elfish light
Fell off in hoary flakes.

By the light of the
Moon he beholdeth
God's creatures of the
great calm.

Within the shadow of the ship
I watched their rich attire:
Blue, glossy green, and velvet black,
They coiled and swam; and every track
Was a flash of golden fire.

O happy living things! no tongue
Their beauty might declare:
A spring of love gushed from my heart,
And I blessed them unaware:
Sure my kind saint took pity on me,
And I blessed them unaware.

Their beauty and
their happiness.

He blesseth them in
his heart.

The self-same moment I could pray;
And from my neck so free
The Albatross fell off, and sank
Like lead into the sea.

The spell begins to
break.

ANONYMOUS

from the Exeter Book
[Riddle]

On earth there's a creature wondrously conceived:
she's wild and unruly, unbridled her momentum;
ferociously she roars as she rolls across the earth.
She has mothered many splendid creatures.
This fair traveller is eager always,
headstrong and inescapable. No one can find
words appropriate to describe to others
her splendid appearance, her innumerable kin,
her ancient origin; the Father saw it all,
the beginning and end, and so did the Son,
sublime child of the Creator . . .
[*lines* 11b–20 *defective or missing*]
This mother is endowed with massive strength;
wondrously sustained, teeming with food
and treasure-adorned, she's dear to men.
Her force increases, her might is revealed,
her grace is enhanced by the great good she offers –
a gift refreshing for proud people,
she's pure and bountiful, boundless her excellence.
She's precious to the rich, useful to the poor,
priceless and freeborn; of all things created
under the sky, on which the sons of men
have set eyes, she's the strongest,
the most strenuous as she covers the ground,
the most grasping and most greedy (so lives
this glorious creature, kinswoman of mortals),
although keen in mind . . .
a more discerning man, a host of marvels.

She's harder than earth, older than heroes,
more generous than gold-givers, dearer than gems;
she beautifies the world, gives birth
to plants, washes away suffering.
From outside, she casts a veil –
a marvellous making – over countless people,
and on earth everywhere men gaze in wonder ...
[*lines 43–56 defective*]

Translated from Old English by Kevin Crossley-Holland

LEIGH HUNT

The Fish, the Man, and the Spirit

To Fish

You strange, astonish'd-looking, angle-faced,
  Dreary-mouth'd, gaping wretches of the sea,
  Gulping salt-water everlastingly,
Cold-blooded, though with red your blood be graced,
And mute, though dwellers in the roaring waste;
  And you, all shapes beside, that fishy be, –
  Some round, some flat, some long, all devilry,
Legless, unloving, infamously chaste: –
O scaly, slippery, wet, swift, staring wights,
  What is't ye do? what life lead? eh, dull goggles?
How do ye vary your vile days and nights?
  How pass your Sundays? Are ye still but joggles
In ceaseless wash? Still nought but gapes and bites,
  And drinks, and stares, diversified with boggles?

A Fish Answers

Amazing monster! that, for aught I know,
  With the first sight of thee didst make our race
  Forever stare! O flat and shocking face,
Grimly divided from the breast below!
Thou that on dry land horribly dost go
  With a split body and most ridiculous pace,
  Prong after prong, disgracer of all grace,
Long-useless-finned, hair'd, upright, unwet, slow!

O breather of unbreathable, sword-sharp air,
  How canst exist? How bear thyself, thou dry
And dreary sloth? What particle canst share
  Of the only blessed life, the watery?
I sometimes see of ye an actual *pair*
  Go by! link'd fin by fin! most odiously.

*The Fish turns into a Man, and then into a Spirit,
and again speaks*

Indulge thy smiling scorn, if smiling still,
  O man! and loathe, but with a sort of love:
  For difference must its use by difference prove,
And, in sweet clang, the spheres with music fill.
One of the spirits am I, that at his will
  Live in whate'er has life – fish, eagle, dove –
  No hate, no pride, beneath nought, nor above,
A visitor of the rounds of God's sweet skill.

Man's life is warm, glad, sad, 'twixt loves and graves,
  Boundless in hope, honour'd with pangs austere,
Heaven-gazing; and his angel-wings he craves:
  The fish is swift, small-needing, vague yet clear,
A cold, sweet, silver life, wrapp'd in round waves,
  Quicken'd with touches of transporting fear.

JOHN BURNSIDE

Salvelinus alpinus

They've troubled me for days, these Arctic charr,
their childish faces cradled in a bowl
of salt and ice, their bodies hatched with night,

muscles of current laid out on a slab,
steel-blue and cold as stone and none of them
singular, none of them real outside the shoal

that maps the tides and wanders with the light
as one long soul: a unity of eyes
and movement, centred everywhere at once

and nowhere, as the centre of the world
is here, and now, in every blade of grass
or poppy head that shivers in the wind,

though when we stop to look, nothing is there,
perfect and cold and snow-blue as this gaze
that shifts from face to face, then disappears.

Who was it said the souls to match our souls
are waiting on the far side of the moon
to take our places, when we step aside?

I never thought to witness such a thing
but these are human faces, human eyes,
human spirits, drifting in the sea

beyond the noise of traffic and the blur
of conversation, one of them my own
replacement, true, but still to be confirmed,

this life beyond the life I have imagined,
livid and slow and dreaming in the tide
with shoals of others, till its time arrives.

EILÉAN NÍ CHUILLEANÁIN

The Sun-Fish
(Other names: Basking shark, An Liamhán Gréine,
Cetorhinus maximus)

1. The watcher

The salmon-nets flung wide, their drift of floats
In a curve ending below the watcher's downward view
From the high promontory. A fin a fluke
And they are there, the huge sun-fish,
Holding still, stencilled in the shallows.

They doze in their long dawdle foraging at edges
Where warmer streams collide with cold, westward.
Their matched shadows trail them up the sound.
What cryptic ocean harboured them since last they surfaced
Out of deep *then?* The late bright evening lies
Flat on the sea, they press up against the glassy screed
Or sink to shades in a delicate layer of smoke.

2. Observations at the surface

Tracking tides, traipsing,
Feeding through their fixed yawn,
They have history, patches,
Warm nights with sudden endings.

The boat was not her measure –
She destroyed the net –
We cut it away and left her
Wounded to death.

Others were sighted
Passing the Seven Heads
And a year later hundreds
Nose to tail off the Lizard.

Where did time leave them?

And again: 'I rounded the corner
In my father's car, they were there,
Exposed, flayed at the quayside,
A bright bloody colour exploded,
Too big for the quay wall,
Too big for the little bay.'

3. Mere peddling

And again: how fast we forget,
How grimy we see the people: men and women,
The clustered stoves on stony beaches, the various tubs and
    barrels
Rendering the oil from the liver, sediment
Settling, useful to curriers, ironfounders
And others. The buyers, the carts waiting;
The voice in each one's head saying *live, live,*
Men able to kill, to impregnate and hunt
In dangerous boats – 'The pale streak over the backbone
Is the place to aim the spear: downward' –
Able to hack cold carcasses and slave
At the hot iron stoves. And when the sun-fish
Were all gone, to crowd the ships for Ayrshire,
Cleveland, Derby. The women's long cry of loss.

4. Their shadow on the sea

Krill. Bloom. Copepods. Elasmobranch. Thermocline. Liamhán
   Gréine
In troops of words they form, a gulp dissolves them.
The ocean swathing the globe is a snake mask.

I watch for the outline, widening the maritime stare.
The angles are a smashed jigsaw. I will not
Let it take shape yet.

I will freeze the dappled light and foam.
But they are already here as the watcher saw them
Then, craning as they nosed in under the cliff,

Suddenly present now, a visitation
Like the faces of my two parents looking at me
From the other side, the outside

Of the misted screen of winter.

SIR JOHN DAVIES

from Orchestra, or a Poeme of Dauncing

For loe the *Sea* that fleets about the Land,
And like a girdle clips her solide waist,
Musicke and measure both doth understand;
For his great chrystall eye is alwayes cast
Up to the Moone, and on her fixèd fast;
  And as she daunceth in her pallid spheere;
  So daunceth he about his Center heere.

Sometimes his proud greene waves in order set,
One after other flow unto the shore;
Which, when they have with many kisses wet,
They ebbe away in order as before;
And to make knowne his courtly love the more,
  He oft doth lay aside his three-forkt mace,
  And with his armes the timorous Earth embrace.

Onely the Earth doth stand for ever still:
Her rocks remove not, nor her mountaines meet:
(Although some wits enricht with Learning's skill
Say heav'n stands firme, and that the Earth doth fleet,
And swiftly turneth underneath their feet)
  Yet though the Earth is ever stedfast seene,
  On her broad breast hath Dauncing ever beene.

For those blew vaines that through her body spred,
Those saphire streames which from great hils do spring.
(The Earth's great duggs; for every wight is fed
With sweet fresh moisture from them issuing):
Observe a daunce in their wilde wandering;
   And still their daunce begets a murmur sweet,
   And still the murmur with the daunce doth meet.

Of all their wayes I love *Maeander's* path,
Which to the tunes of dying swans doth daunce;
Such winding sleights, such turns and tricks he hath,
Such creeks, such wrenches, and such daliaunce;
That whether it be hap or heedlesse chaunce,
   In this indented course and wriggling play
   He seemes to daunce a perfect cunning *hay*.

But wherefore doe these streames for ever runne?
To keepe themselves for ever sweet and cleere:
For let their everlasting course be donne,
They straight corrupt and foule with mud appeare.
O yee sweet Nymphs that beautie's losse do feare,
   Contemne the drugs that Physicke doth devise,
   And learne of Love this dainty exercise.

See how those flowres that have sweet beauty too,
(The onely jewels that the Earth doth weare,
When the young Sunne in bravery her doth woo):
As oft as they the whistling wind doe heare,
Doe wave their tender bodies here and there;
   And though their daunce no perfect measure is,
   Yet oftentimes their musicke makes them kis.

What makes the vine about the elme to daunce,
With turnings, windings, and embracements round?
What makes the loadstone to the North advance
His subtile point, as if from thence he found
His chiefe attractive vertue to redound?
   Kind Nature first doth cause all things to love,
   Love makes them daunce and in just order move.

Harke how the birds doe sing, and marke then how
Jumpe with the modulation of their layes,
They lightly leape, and skip from bow to bow:
Yet doe the cranes deserve a greater prayse
Which keepe such measure in their ayrie wayes,
   As when they all in order rankèd are,
   They make a perfect forme triangular.

In the chiefe angle flyes the watchfull guid,
And all the followers their heads doe lay
On their foregoers backs, on eyther side;
But for the captaine hath no rest to stay,
His head forewearied with the windy way,
   He back retires, and then the next behind,
   As his lieuetenaunt leads them through the wind.

CHASE TWICHELL

The Rule of the North Star

I should be ashamed to love
the first hard frost the way I do,

the way it glitters
over the surface of everything,

erasing whatever's human.

But I'm not. So I stand for a minute
in the crystalline grass
with an armload of frozen firewood,

letting a little of the ruthlessness
enter my bones, breathing
white sparrows into the air.

Oh, I know where the logic leads.
If the lights of the town

spoil the dark ... If the trucks
downshifting on the Cascade hill
infect the wind ...

If humanity's the enemy, the enemy is me.

But there's something in me, an arrow
that points toward wilderness,

toward the mountain that governs
such loves, its ledges high enough
to have caught last night's

faint halo of snow.
Wherever I am, in all weathers,
I look up, and it's there,

it always has been, rising even
above the charred towers of cities,
under the north star which glints down

onto its sharp summit,
and onto each withered grass blade,

each rattling pod, each burned-out-car,
each smaller star of broken glass.

The mountain which has no name
burns in the distance

with a beautiful, radical plainness,

ledges bright with snowmelt.
It's the shrine,

the afterimage of the moment in which
I first imagined the world's death,

and knew at the same stroke
that though it would survive in some form,

it would not survive in this form.

The firewood aches in my arms.
Its smoke will cross over,

touching both the ash in the fireplace
and the face of the mirage.

The north star
comes out earlier each evening.

It shines down onto the cloudy
or snowy or clear-skied world,

the wars, the droughts, the famines,

the ethnic cleansings,
just as it shone on the plagues,

the witch trials, the forced marches,
the purges, the great extinctions.

It will still be the sharpest spark
in the heavens long after my death,

your death, the next death of language —

a spark that will preside over the world
we leave behind, where acres of bones

catch the starlight, and a gray wind
scribbles in the drifts of ash.

JENNIFER ATKINSON

The End of Advent

Free verse

      An ice storm glints
On the cinder path and the pear tree,
                        on the clothesline
In its chaste majesty,
And the red-flagged mailboxes bunched on the corner.
Cold as clean as dry sugar
Tastes granular on the tongue. Brilliance
                      like buckshot stings
Everywhere at once –
            hark, hark, hark:
The seen world as ever shines ...

Sometimes, in winter, when the ice-sheathed barbs of the holly
Glare as they do now,
And the spruce stands tall enough to stand for something
At the frozen back garden's verge,
                 I catch myself dreaming
Down the pollarded steeple on the old Haddam church,
Burnt and rebuilt. I remember the way
               the deacons' wives
Whited out
        with lilies its fat altar cross at Easter,
The pollen on the petals, the tassels on the flags,
The Allelulias and Risens, the organ
             declaring a 'victory won.'

Reverend McLared, who bent tree roots
Into gnarled, elegant walking sticks

And put up great batches of concord wine jelly

                      in his spare time,

Labored to ease our mind
With John's 'Whosoever believeth, etc.,'
Words he regretted, he told us at dinner,
Having preached in Burma decades before.

I drive out to the end of Filley Road where the cracked
Macadam narrows and the forest officially starts,
Where mountain laurel,

                  wind-stunted, ice-lacquered,

Slaps at the car-doors,

               and head in a ways

Past the frozen fire pond, a picnic site, a pine stand
So shady that even in summer a wintry gloom

                         persists.

There's nobody else around.

                So who's to mind

If I sing to the pine and hardwood

                 solitude a carol

Gapped

        and bridged with botched, forgotten, and made-up words?

The sign's down, but I know the place
By its over-and-gone

               and set-apart look:

Stone fences in a rubble, a rusty loop
Of barbed wire in a clearing
Lapped with the wax-green fern they call Christmas.

It's been thirty years since I was last here.
Forty since anyone stoked the fires or shovelled the ash
At the Cockaponsett Charcoal Works and yet,

                    under a deadfall,

A broken white birch,

twiggy and tinseled with icicles,
I unearth a heap of half-burnt logs,
load a couple into the car,
Wipe my charry hands on my shirt for the sheer pleasure of it,
And, cold or not,
do not yet turn homeward.

Tomorrow will be Christmas Day.

There's no such thing as silence in the woods.
But through the sheer unsteady wind, jays, and way-off
A ranger's chain saw,
I hear a footfall,
another, and turn.
The doe, faded dun, nervous
– no ghost –
Startles and crashes back among the shadowed trees
As is she were the stranger.

The world is no Advent calendar, its days
Gilt doors marked with cardinal numbers and symbols:
Holly, lily, charcoal, deer
To be prized open, one by one,
a lesson in patience.

And who would prefer it were so?

DYLAN THOMAS

'The force that through the green fuse drives the flower'

The force that through the green fuse drives the flower
Drives my green age; that blasts the roots of trees
Is my destroyer.
And I am dumb to tell the crooked rose
My youth is bent by the same wintry fever.

The force that drives the water through the rocks
Drives my red blood; that dries the mouthing streams
Turns mine to wax.
And I am dumb to mouth unto my veins
How at the mountain spring the same mouth sucks.

The hand that whirls the water in the pool
Stirs the quicksand; that ropes the blowing wind
Hauls my shroud sail.
And I am dumb to tell the hanging man
How of my clay is made the hangman's lime.

The lips of time leech to the fountain head;
Love drips and gathers, but the fallen blood
Shall calm her sores.
And I am dumb to tell a weather's wind
How time has ticked a heaven round the stars.

And I am dumb to tell the lover's tomb
How at my sheet goes the same crooked worm.

PERCY BYSSHE SHELLEY

Ode to the West Wind

O wild West Wind, thou breath of Autumn's being,
Thou, from whose unseen presence the leaves dead
Are driven, like ghosts from an enchanter fleeing,

Yellow, and black, and pale, and hectic red,
Pestilence-stricken multitudes: O thou,
Who chariotest to their dark wintry bed

The wingèd seeds, where they lie cold and low,
Each like a corpse within its grave, until
Thine azure sister of the Spring shall blow

Her clarion o'er the dreaming earth, and fill
(Driving sweet buds like flocks to feed in air)
With living hues and odours plain and hill:

Wild Spirit, which art moving everywhere;
Destroyer and preserver; hear, oh, hear!

Thou on whose streams, mid the steep sky's commotion,
Loose clouds like earth's decaying leaves are shed,
Shook from the tangled boughs of Heaven and Ocean,

Angels of rain and lightning: there are spread
On the blue surface of thine aëry surge,
Like the bright hair uplifted from the head

Of some fierce Maenad, even from the dim verge
Of the horizon to the zenith's height,
The locks of the approaching storm. Thou dirge

Of the dying year, to which this closing night
Will be the dome of a vast sepulchre,
Vaulted with all thy congregated might

Of vapours, from whose solid atmosphere
Black rain, and fire, and hail will burst: oh, hear!

Thou who didst waken from his summer dreams
The blue Mediterranean, where he lay,
Lulled by the coil of his crystàlline streams,

Beside a pumice isle in Baiae's bay,
And saw in sleep old palaces and towers
Quivering within the wave's intenser day,

All overgrown with azure moss and flowers
So sweet, the sense faints picturing them! Thou
For whose path the Atlantic's level powers

Cleave themselves into chasms, while far below
The sea-blooms and the oozy woods which wear
The sapless foliage of the ocean, know

Thy voice, and suddenly grow gray with fear,
And tremble and despoil themselves: oh, hear!

If I were a dead leaf thou mightest bear;
If I were a swift cloud to fly with thee;
A wave to pant beneath thy power, and share

The impulse of thy strength, only less free
Than thou, O uncontrollable! If even
I were as in my boyhood, and could be

The comrade of thy wanderings over Heaven,
As then, when to outstrip thy skiey speed
Scarce seemed a vision; I would ne'er have striven

As thus with thee in prayer in my sore need.
Oh, lift me as a wave, a leaf, a cloud!
I fall upon the thorns of life! I bleed!

A heavy weight of hours has chained and bowed
One too like thee: tameless, and swift, and proud.

Make me thy lyre, even as the forest is:
What if my leaves are falling like its own!
The tumult of thy mighty harmonies

Will take from both a deep, autumnal tone,
Sweet though in sadness. Be thou, Spirit fierce,
My spirit! Be thou me, impetuous one!

Drive my dead thoughts over the universe
Like withered leaves to quicken a new birth!
And, by the incantation of this verse,

Scatter, as from an unextinguished hearth
Ashes and sparks, my words among mankind!
Be through my lips to unawakened earth

The trumpet of a prophecy! O, Wind,
If Winter comes, can Spring be far behind?

D. M. BLACK

For and Against the Environment

I have come out to smell the hyacinths which again in this
   North London garden

have performed a wonderful feat of chemistry and hauled that
   delectable perfume

out of the blackish confection of clay and potsherds which
   feebly responds when I name it flower-bed;

and so wet was the Spring that I clipped the grass with shears,
   to prevent the mower sliding in mud,

and my attempt to dig the beds to enhance their fertility
   foundered caked with clods.

But today the April sun blazes from a cloudless sky, and the
   lawn, drenched with raindrops

like an utterly saturated sponge has unfurled and surrendered its
   freight,

and – where do they come from? – the small pert insects
   emerge onto the skin of dryness

like Noah's prospecting pigeon and at once they are up to all
   sorts of business,

and the buds you had thought paralysed if not embalmed are
   surely discernibly plumper

and purpler or pinker than you remember them yesterday, and
the hum of potential life

swells with its distinctive excitement to just short of the
threshold of actual audibility

through which it bursts, perhaps, by way of the throat of that
unceasing ingenious blackbird

poised on my neighbour's gutter against the blue of the sky. O,
wonderful world!

and here are two absolute flowers, new as babies:

they have bowed their heads for weeks in their bashful, fleecy
pods,

but today they stare up at me bravely, giving all they have got

and making at last no pretence they are anything else but
anemones

and this is their hour, and if they don't impress now they will
never impress,

but they do, and to support my judgment a small fly is
clambering deliberately over the organ stops of their stamens

making, I do not doubt, marvellous music. O, wonderful world!

And the ant is rushing at immense speed over the lifeless plains
of the rose-bed

which are not plains to her but ridged and crested with salts
and terrible canyons

and she winds every which way through them but never forgets
her sense of direction

for she is not such a fool as to think, but attends to the sun and
the earth's magnetism

and I am shocked by my own thought, that my own thought

may be a blind lobe on the body of the great creature of
evolution,

an experiment which does not carry the future. And meanwhile
here is this ant,

only the most distant relation of Mozart and Shakespeare, yet
unmistakably designed for survival,

nosing about through the clods like an exceptionally fleet piece
of earth-moving equipment

and not in the least reciprocating the warm concern she has
evoked in me,

and the same is true of the blackbird, whose song I salute, and
the anemone

whose sleek pods I have fondled, and the clods which I have
rendered more fertile,

and at this moment, speaking now as one of the Lords of
Creation,

speaking as one of the Shepherds of Being, unique bearers of
conscious and self-conscious life,

I have to declare my preference within all the sparkling welter

(O, wonderful world!) and I do, keeping the ant firmly fixed in
   my gaze:

great and more fragile is man than ant or earth or anemone

and in or out of the glass-house of nature, let him above all not
   be seduced.

EDMUND SPENSER

from The Faerie Queene
[The Garden of Adonis]

In that same Gardin all the goodly flowres,
   Wherewith dame Nature doth her beautifie,
   and decks the girlonds of her paramoures,
   Are fetcht: there is the first seminarie
   Of all things, that are borne to live and die,
   According to their kindes. Long worke it were,
   Here to account the endlesse progenie
   Of all the weedes, that bud and blossome there;
But so much as doth need, must needs be counted here.

It sited was in fruitfull soyle of old,
   And girt in with two walles on either side;
   The one of yron, the other of bright gold,
   That none might thorough breake, nor over-stride:
   And double gates it had, which opened wide,
   By which both in and out men moten pas;
   Th'one faire and fresh, the other old and dride:
   Old *Genius* the porter of them was,
Old *Genius*, the which a double nature has.

He letteth in, he letteth out to wend,
   All that to come into the world desire;
   A thousand thousand naked babes attend
   About him day and night, which doe require,
   That he with fleshly weedes would them attire:
   Such as him list, such as eternall fate
   Ordained hath, he clothes with sinfull mire,

And sendeth forth to live in mortall state,
Till they againe returne backe by the hinder gate.

After that they againe returned beene,
    They in that Gardin planted be againe;
    And grow afresh, as they had never seene
    Fleshly corruption, nor mortall paine.
    Some thousand yeares so doen they there remaine;
    And then of him are clad with other hew,
    Or sent into the chaungefull world againe,
    Till thither they returne, where first they grew:
So like a wheele around they runne from old to new.

Ne needs there Gardiner to set, or sow,
    To plant or prune: for of their owne accord
    All things, as they created were, doe grow,
    And yet remember well the mightie word,
    Which first was spoken by th'Almightie lord,
    That bad them to increase and multiply:
    Ne doe they need with water of the ford,
    Or of the clouds to moysten their roots dry;
For in themselves eternall moisture they imply.

Infinite shapes of creatures there are bred,
    And uncouth formes, which none yet ever knew,
    And every sort is in a sundry bed
    Set by it selfe, and ranckt in comely rew:
    Some fit for reasonable soules t'indew,
    Some made for beasts, some made for birds to weare,
    And all the fruitfull spawne of fishes hew
    In endlesse rancks along enraunged were,
That seem'd the *Ocean* could not containe them there.

Daily they grow, and daily forth are sent
  Into the world, it to replenish more;
  Yet is the stocke not lessened, nor spent,
  But still remaines in everlasting store,
  As it at first created was of yore.
  For in the wide wombe of the world there lyes,
  In hatefull darkenesse and in deepe horrore,
  An huge eternall *Chaos*, which supplyes
The substance of natures fruitfull progenyes.

All things from thence doe their first being fetch,
  And borrow matter, whereof they are made,
  Which when as forme and feature it does ketch,
  Becomes a bodie, and doth then invade
  The state of life, out of the griesly shade.
  That substance is eterne, and bideth so,
  Ne when the life decayes, and forme does fade,
  Doth it consume, and into nothing go,
But chaunged is, and often altred to and fro.

The substance is not chaunged, nor altered,
  But th'only forme and outward fashion;
  For every substance is conditioned
  To change her hew, and sundry formes to don,
  Meet for her temper and complexion:
  For formes are variable and decay,
  By course of kind, and by occasion;
  And that faire flowre of beautie fades away,
As doth the lilly fresh before the sunny ray.

Great enimy to it, and to all the rest,
  That in the *Gardin* of *Adonis* springs,
  Is wicked *Time*, who with his scyth addrest,
  Does mow the flowring herbes and goodly things,
  And all their glory to the ground downe flings,

Where they doe wither, and are fowly mard:
He flyes about, and with his flaggy wings
Beates down both leaves and buds without regard,
Ne ever pittie may relent his malice hard.

Yet pittie often did the gods relent,
　　To see so faire things mard, and spoyled quight:
　　And their great mother *Venus* did lament
　　The losse of her deare brood, her deare delight;
　　Her hart was pierst with pittie at the sight,
　　When walking through the Gardin, them she spyde,
　　Yet no'te she find redresse for such despight.
　　For all that lives, is subject to that law:
All things decay in time, and to their end do draw.

But were it not, that *Time* their troubler is,
　　All that in this delightful Gardin growes,
　　Should happie be, and have immortall blis:
　　For here all plentie, and all pleasure flowes,
　　And sweet love gentle fits emongst them throwes,
　　Without fell rancor, or fond gealosie;
　　Franckly each paramour his leman knowes,
　　Each bird his mate, ne any does envie
Their goodly meriment, and gay felicitie.

There is continuall spring, and harvest there
　　Continuall, both meeting at one time:
　　For both the boughes doe laughing blossomes beare,
　　And with fresh colours decke the wanton Prime,
　　And eke attonce the heavy trees they clime,
　　Which seeme to labour under their fruits lode:
　　The whiles the joyous birdes make their pastime
　　Emongst the shadie leaves, their sweet abode,
And their true loves without suspition tell abrode.

JOHN KEATS

On the Grasshopper and Cricket

The poetry of earth is never dead:
When all the birds are faint with the hot sun,
   And hide in cooling trees, a voice will run
From hedge to hedge about the new-mown mead.
That is the Grasshopper's – he takes the lead
   In summer luxury, – he has never done
   With his delights; for when tired out with fun,
He rests at ease beneath some pleasant weed.
The poetry of earth is ceasing never:
   On a lone winter evening, when the frost
      Has wrought a silence, from the stove there shrills
The Cricket's song, in warmth increasing ever,
   And seems to one in drowsiness half lost,
      The Grasshopper's among some grassy hills.

CHARLES WRIGHT

Meditation on Summer and Shapelessness

We have a bat, one bat, that bug-surfs
                              our late-summer back yard
Just as the fireflies begin
To rise, new souls, toward the August moon.
Flap-limbed, ungathered,
He stumbles unerringly through them,
Exempt as they feint and ascend to their remission –
Light, Catharist light;
Brightness to brightness where I sit
                        on the back brink of my sixth decade,
Virginia moon in the cloud-ragged, cloud-scutted sky,
Bat bug-drawn and swallow-crossed, God's wash.

One comes to understand
                        Candide and Tiberius,
Sour saints, aspiring aphasiacs,
Recluses and anchorites,
Those whom the moon's pull and the moon's
                                    hydrointerpretation
Crumble twice under,
Those hard few for whom the Eagle has never landed.
Out here, all's mythic, medieval, or early A.D.
One half expects
            Raymond of Toulouse or Hadrian to step forth,
Resplendent and otherwise, out of the hedge row or arborvitae.
One half hopes, moon's gun with a dead bead.

————

I never quite got it, what they meant,
                              but now I do,
Waking each morning at dawn,
Or before, some shapeless, unfingerprintable dread
On me like cold-crossed humidity,
Extinction shouldering, like a season, in from my dreamscape.
Without my glasses, the light around the window shade
Throbs like an aura, so faint
At first, then luminous with its broken promises –
Feckless icon, dark reliquary.
Mortality hunches, like fine furniture, crowding the room.

Rising, feeding the dogs, bringing the newspaper in,
Somehow should loosen things up.
It doesn't, of course.
                         There's still the pill to be taken,
And then another, eye drops,
Toothbrush and toothpaste,
                              reflection of someone older and strange
Constantly in the mirror,
Breakfast and then the day's doom, long-leafed
And everywhere,
Shadowing what I look at, shadowing what I see.
The News, then supper, then back to the black beginning.

———————

Après-dog days, dead end of August,
Summer a holding pattern,
                              heat, haze, humidity
The mantra we still chant, the bell-tick our tongues all toll.
Whatever rises becomes a light –
Firefly and new moon,
Star and star and star chart
                              unscrolled across the heavens
Like radioactive dump sites bulb-lit on a map.

Whatever holds back goes dark –
The landscape and all its accoutrements, my instinct, my hands,
My late, untouchable hands.

Summer's crepuscular, rot and wrack,
Rain-ravaged, root-ruined.
Each August the nightscape inserts itself
                                    another inch in my heart,
Piece and a piece, piecemeal, time's piecework.
August unedges and polishes me, water's way.
Such subtle lapidary.
Last lights go out in the next-door house,
                                    dogs disappear,
Privet and white pine go under, bird-squelch and frog-shrill.
To be separate, to be apart, is to be whole again.
Full night now and dust-sheet –
                        the happy life is the darkened life.

JOY HARJO

Summer Night

The moon is nearly full,
                  the humid air sweet like melon.
Flowers that have cupped the sun all day
                         dream of iridescent wings
under the long dark sleep.
                  Children's invisible voices call out
in the glimmering moonlight.
                    Their parents play worn-out records
of the cumbia. Behind the screen door
                  their soft laughter swells
into the rhythm of a smooth guitar.
                I watch the world shimmer
inside this globe of a summer night,
                listen to the wobble of her
spin and dive. It happens all the time, waiting for you
                    to come home
There is an ache that begins
                in the sound of an old blues song.
It becomes a house where all the lights have gone out
                  but one.
And it burns and burns
                until there is only the blue smoke of dawn
and everyone is sleeping in someone's arms
                even the flowers
even the sound of a thousand silences.
              And the arms of night
in the arms of day.
          Everyone except me.
But then the smell of damp honeysuckle twisted on the vine.

And the turn of the shoulder
                    of the ordinary spirit who keeps watch
over this ordinary street.
                    And there you are, the secret
of your own flower of light
                    blooming in the miraculous dark.

ANGELA SORBY

Empire Builder
Chicago–Seattle, 1995

Where do the buffalo roam? Once,
the West was a playfield

for pioneers, who saw money bleeding
from the great creatures' ears.

They shot them by the million
from this route, so now it's tame:

a country of doves and sage.
My husband spotted a buffalo,

or did he dream it? I don't know.
The past is a closed drawer.

Maybe there really were angels
circling the Great Salt Lake

in Brigham Young's day,
but their wings are snipped at the root

and folded, private as underwear.
They won't block the track. No

turning back: tonight we'll pass
Glacier Park in the dark,

on a trestle so high the sleeping
bears won't rouse. Remote

as a meteor traversing Ursa Major,
we'll push west to Seattle,

to our house, to our bed in the red
cedar basement, to our St Francis

night light burning with power
from rivers full of dead salmon

trapped by dams. St Francis's feet
and fingers flood the room with faux fire:

this is how we live, with our bones
in blood, at the end of the empire.

Notes on the Commissioned Poems

Simon Armitage on 'The Final Straw', p. 149
I was thinking of what is known in economic geography as 'The tragedy of the commons'. Rich farmland is plundered until it is utterly exhausted. In the poem, the reapers take part in an ancient fertility ceremony, but out of the last few grains flies a Spix's Macaw. Can there be a more potent omen of the dying planet than this bird, whose world population is reckoned to be just one?

John Burnside on 'Salvelinus alpinus', p. 210
I worked with the botanist Elisabeth Cooper, fully intending to write very specifically about sub-Arctic flora, in particular the Arctic poppy (which appears at the centre of the poem). In the end, the Arctic charr made an unexpected appearance, after an eerie encounter in a Tromsø fish market, so the plant references, while still central, gave way, on the surface at least, to fish (something of a pet theme for me).

Mark Doty on 'Flit', p. 151
'Flit' began with a small flock of black-capped chickadees, *Poecile atricapalla*. (Doesn't that 'Poecile' link them immediately to poetry?) One winter afternoon on a walk in a beech forest near Provincetown, Massachusetts, at the end of Cape Cod, I felt intensely observed by the little birds, and fascinated by the way they seemed to make decisions collectively about direction and intent. I turned to Robert Finch, a Cape Cod naturalist (whose books of essays include *Death of a Hornet*) and a remarkable source of information on bird life in New England.

Paul Farley on 'An Ovaltine Tin in the Egg Collections at Tring', p. 134
This poem is dedicated to Michael Walters on his retirement as Curator of Eggs; who, at one stage, I had rummaging through the

tins and boxes used to house amateur egg collections. It looks as though I've tried to curate these ancillary objects, and to place the smaller, faster world of tins and commerce in some kind of relation to the bigger, older world of eggshell and birdsong.

Allison Funk on 'Ephemeroptera', p. 53
To help me with my poem, my brother, David Funk, an entomologist specialising in aquatic insects, sent me some amazing photos he had taken of mayflies. It wasn't, however, until he used metaphors to describe them – 'snowstorm', 'smoke' – that I could see them emerging in thousands from rivers and streams. I started my poem there.

Linda Gregerson on 'Elegant', p. 91
In 2002, the Nobel Prize in Physiology was awarded to Sydney Brenner, Robert Horvitz and John Sulston for discoveries concerning 'genetic regulation of organ development and programmed cell death'. *C. elegans* is the model organism they used in their research. My thanks to Nelson Horseman for calling my attention to this beautiful work, to John Sulston for sharing with me the text of his Nobel lecture, and, above all, to Ron Ellis for his patient and generous tutelage.

Seamus Heaney on 'On the Spot', p. 161
One of the pleasures of staying at The Wood, a small farm owned by an aunt and uncle on my father's side, was going out every morning to collect the eggs from laying boxes in the henhouse. But we were always on the lookout for hens that were 'laying away' and the poem recalls a 'spot of time' when that search yielded particularly memorable results.

James Lasdun on 'A Peeled Wand', p. 121
This is a poem about a cross-species encounter that stirred me. It is more a collaboration with an animal than with a scientist. I did however have illuminating conversations with Kristine

Flones, a Wildlife Rehabilitator here in the Catskills, who confirmed to me that what I had observed was entirely in keeping with the behaviour of beavers.

Andrew Motion on 'Sparrow', p. 143

I wrote 'Sparrow' adapting an Anglo-Saxon verse form I found in *The Rattle Bag*, and wanted to invite readers to consider the plight of all kinds of endangered species – the humble as well as the exotic. In the opening lines I tried to evoke country sparrows, in the middle part I looked at town sparrows, and in the final section I tried to capture the sparrowness of sparrows wherever they are (or are not any more).

Paul Muldoon on 'Glaucus', p. 75

I was drawn to the subject of Glaucus largely because of his story's dramatisation of the notion of 'what comes around goes around', or is it 'what goes around comes around'? I think of him particularly in the context of bovine spongiform encephalitis, and the other manifestations of enforced cannibalism such as feeding chickens chicken shit.

Eiléan Ní Chuilleanáin on 'The Sun-Fish', p. 212

The poem grew out of an assembly of memories and atmospheres: childhood holidays on the Galway coast and islands, T.H. Mason's *The Islands of Ireland*, which fascinated me in childhood, memories of my contemporaries including my husband, Macdara Woods, who had seen basking sharks in Achill, and marine biologist Jim O'Meara who encountered one when fishing with a drift net at his home in West Cork. My grandmother gave me *The Sea Around Us* when it was first published but it was only when I went back and read Carson's work last year that I realised how much she had influenced my thinking all my life.

Deryn Rees-Jones on 'Trilobite', p. 199
Richard Fortey's enthusiasm, his ability to write like a poet whilst thinking like a scientist, left me wanting to know more about these small creatures. He made me realise that while these fossils may be key to an understanding of the animal kingdom they are also, in his words, 'imbued with all the tawdry and magnificent stuff of human lives'.

Christopher Reid on 'A Pub Band', p. 173
This poem is the product of ignorance, or easily defeated intelligence. Reading around the subject of the genesis of the solar system I found myself repeatedly running up against mathematical formulae beyond my grasp. I then began to wonder if creation myths and proper scientific knowledge could speak to each other in any profitable way. Sir John Davies's glorious, energetic poem 'Orchestra' (1596), which perceives the whole of nature dancing to a heavenly music, rose to the challenge of his day. The best I could come up with was a lurching pub band.

Maurice Riordan on 'The January Birds', p. 45
The poem was prompted by looking at the phenological charts of the Woodland Trust (which record seasonal change in the UK). It occurred to me that the signs of spring, which are traditionally so heartening, can nowadays seem ominous indicators of climate change. Some of the birds in the poem sing out of season.

Robin Robertson on 'Primavera', p. 44
In March 2003, while I was working in a tower in Santa Maddalena, an hour east of Florence, my younger daughter (to whom the poem is dedicated) was at home in London, turning ten. I have been a little flexible with the phenological facts, but the poem is, in essence, accurate. If global temperatures are allowed to increase at the current rate, when Cait is my age spring will arrive a fortnight earlier than it does today.

Michael Symmons Roberts on 'To John Donne', p. 79

'To John Donne' came out of a series of conversations with Sir John Sulston, head of the team that mapped the genome at the Sanger Centre in Cambridge. That conversation was both a privilege and an inspiration, since John – as father of the map – is passionately concerned that his work should not be abused. In particular, he has grave concerns – as do I – about genetic patenting. There's a clear analogy with the history of the land here. Unmapped, the human body was a common ground for all of us. Now, big business is seeking to patent parts of our common genome for their own profit. Taking its bearings from 'To His Mistress Going To Bed', the poem is about the mapping and ownership of the body. The gene code in the final stanza is from the BRCA1 gene, already a patenting battleground because of its connections with some forms of breast cancer.

Robert Wrigley on 'The Gift of the Bear', p. 189

Professor Charles Robbins invited me to Washington State University's Bear Research Center. I watched Dr Robbins and his assistants – was even allowed to help – as they anaesthetised a number of bears for pre-hibernation blood draws. These are grizzly bears: *Ursus arctos horribilis*. By the time I left, I reeked of bears. There was a smear of grizzly blood on my hand. The bears my wife and I see sometimes on our land are black bears, not grizzlies. But the presence of bears where we live keeps us a little more alive than we might be otherwise

Acknowledgements

Poems commissioned for this anthology: © 2004 SIMON ARMITAGE 'The Final Straw' (p. 149), JOHN BURNSIDE 'Salvelinus alpinus' (p. 210), MARK DOTY 'Flit' (p. 151), PAUL FARLEY 'An Ovaltine Tin in the Egg Collections at Tring' (p. 134), ALLISON FUNK 'Ephemeroptera' (p. 53), LINDA GREGERSON 'Elegant' (p. 91), SEAMUS HEANEY 'On the Spot' (p. 161), JAMES LASDUN 'A Peeled Wand' (p. 121), ANDREW MOTION 'Sparrow' (p. 143), PAUL MULDOON 'Glaucus' (p. 75), EILÉAN NÍ CHUILLEANÁIN 'The Sun-Fish' (p. 212), DERYN REES-JONES 'Trilobite' (p. 199), CHRISTOPHER REID 'A Pub Band' (p.173), MAURICE RIORDAN 'The January Birds' (p. 45), ROBIN ROBERTSON 'Primavera' (p. 44), MICHAEL SYMMONS ROBERTS 'To John Donne' (p. 79), ROBERT WRIGLEY 'The Gift of the Bear' (p.189).

The editors and publishers gratefully acknowledge permission to reprint copyright material in this book as follows:

A.R. AMMONS 'Corsons Inlet', copyright © 1963 A.R. Ammons, from *Collected Poems 1951–1971*, reprinted by permission of W.W. Norton & Company, Inc.

SIMON ARMITAGE translation of 'Gawain's Journey North' from *Sir Gawain and the Green Knight*, copyright © 2004 Simon Armitage, published by kind permission of the author.

JENNIFER ATKINSON 'The End of Advent' from *The Drowned City*, copyright © 2000 Jennifer Atkinson, reprinted by permission of Northeastern University Press.

W.H. AUDEN 'Ode to Gaea' from *Collected Poems*, 2004, reprinted by permission of Faber and Faber Ltd.

ELIZABETH BISHOP 'The Armadillo' from *The Complete Poems: 1927–1979*, copyright © 1979, 1983 Alice Helen Methfessel, reprinted by permission of Farrar, Straus and Giroux, LLC.

D.M. BLACK 'For and Against the Environment' from *Collected Poems 1964–87*, published by Polygon, 1991, reprinted by permission of Birlinn Ltd.

BILLY COLLINS 'As if to Demonstrate an Eclipse' from *Nine Horses*, published by Picador, 2003, reprinted by permission of Pan Macmillan Ltd, London.

ROBERT CRAWFORD 'The Bad Shepherd' from *The Tip of My Tongue*, published by Jonathan Cape, 2003, reprinted by permission of The Random House Group Limited.

KEVIN CROSSLEY-HOLLAND translation of 'Riddle' from *The Exeter Book of Riddles*, copyright © Kevin Crossley-Holland, published by Penguin

Books, 1979, reprinted by permission of the author, c/o Rogers, Coleridge & White Ltd., 20 Powis Mews, London WII IJN.

JAMES DICKEY 'The Heaven of Animals' from *The Whole Motion: Collected Poems, 1945–1992*, reprinted by permission of Wesleyan University Press.

JAMES FENTON 'The Orange Dove of Fiji' from *Out of Danger*, published by Penguin, 1993, reprinted by permission of PFD on behalf of James Fenton.

ROBERT FROST 'To a Moth Seen in Winter'; 'Two Look at Two' from *The Poetry of Robert Frost*, edited by Edward Connery Lathem and published by Jonathan Cape, 2001, reprinted by permission of the Estate of Robert Frost and The Random House Group Limited.

JORIE GRAHAM 'Love' from *Erosion*, 1983, reprinted by permission of Carcanet Press Limited.

LAVINIA GREENLAW 'The Recital of Lost Cities' from *Night Photograph*, 1993, reprinted by permission of Faber and Faber Ltd.

JOY HARJO 'Summer Night' from *In Mad Love and War*, 1990, reprinted by permission of Wesleyan University Press.

SEAMUS HEANEY 'St Kevin and the Blackbird' from *The Spirit Level*, 2001, reprinted by permission of Faber and Faber Ltd.

TED HUGHES 'October Salmon' from *River*, 1983, reprinted by permission of Faber and Faber Ltd.

KATHLEEN JAMIE 'Crossing the Loch' from *Jizzen*, 1999, reprinted by permission of Macmillan, London.

ROBINSON JEFFERS 'Carmel Point' from *Selected Poems*, 1987, reprinted by permission of Carcanet Press Limited.

RODNEY JONES 'The Assault on the Fields' from *Elegy for the Southern Drawl*, copyright © 1999 Rodney Jones, reprinted by permission of Houghton Mifflin Company, all rights reserved.

GALWAY KINNELL 'Saint Francis and the Sow' from *Mortal Acts, Mortal Words*, copyright © 1980 Galway Kinnell, reprinted by permission of Houghton Mifflin Company, all rights reserved.

PHILIP LARKIN 'Going, Going' from *Collected Poems*, 2001, reprinted by permission of Faber and Faber Ltd.

D.H. LAWRENCE 'Snake' from *The Complete Poems*, copyright © 1964, 1971 Angelo Ravagli and C.M. Weekley, executors of the estate of Frieda Lawrence Ravagli, published by Penguin, 1994, reprinted by permission of Pollinger Limited and the proprietor.

NORMAN MACCAIG 'Toad' from *Collected Poems*, published by Chatto & Windus, 1993, reprinted by permission of The Random House Group Limited.

JAMIE MCKENDRICK 'Right of Way' from *Ink Stone*, 2003, reprinted by permission of Faber and Faber Ltd.

W.S. MERWIN 'Visitation' from *Opening The Hand*, published by Atheneum, 1983.

Index of Poets